JOHN F. KENNEDY

Roth, Mark.
796.6   Bicycling through England / by Mark
Roth and Sally Walters. New York : H. Z.
Walck, c1976.
    vii, 130 p., [1] leaf of plates : ill.
:

    Bibliography: p. 120-121. Includes in-
dex. Guide to bicycling through England
covering bicycles, itineraries, and
lodgings. Reference sections of additional information, maps, and suppliers.

    1.Cycling-Great Britain
    I.Walters, Sally, jt. auth.
II.Title   75-43038
796.6   GV1046.G7R67

BICYCLING
THROUGH ENGLAND

BICYCLING THROUGH ENGLAND

by Mark Roth and Sally Walters

illustrated with photographs

Henry Z. Walck, Inc.
A DIVISION OF
David McKay Company, Inc.
NEW YORK

LIBRARY OF CONGRESS CATALOGING IN PUBLICATION DATA

Roth, Mark.
  Bicycling through England.

  Bibliography: p.
  Includes index.
  SUMMARY: Guide to bicycling through England
covering bicycles, itineraries, and lodgings.
Reference sections of additional information, maps,
and suppliers.
  1. Cycling—Great Britain—Juvenile literature.
[1. Bicycles and bicycling—Great Britain]
I. Walters, Sally, joint author. II. Title.
GV1046.G7R67   796.6   75-43038
ISBN 0-8098-5004-4
ISBN 0-8098-5009-5 pbk.

Contents

Authors' Note

We have tried to keep our discussion of costs up with current prices, but we cannot guarantee that all figures are still correct. In converting from British to United States currency, the pound sterling has been given a value of $2.30. As the exchange rate has fluctuated greatly in recent years, this is only an approximation. Figures have often been rounded off for simplification.

The authors wish to take this opportunity to thank some of the people who aided them and made their work easier. Merrily Dodson cheerfully proofread the typescript. The photographs which appear here were printed with the generous assistance of Vincent H. Vilardo. And June Kear of the British Tourist Authority has been most kind in answering our queries and helping us to check on details.

N

SCOTLAND

Lake
District

Yorkshire

WALES

ENGLAND

East
Anglia

Cotswolds

Somerset

LONDON

Wessex

Surrey

Kent

Sussex

Devon

Cornwall

0   25   50   100 miles

BICYCLING
THROUGH ENGLAND

1/What It's Like

Who should cycle in England? Anyone who really wants to get to know it—to see how its people live, to know where its wealth is and isn't, to see what its poets and painters and naturalists saw, to see where its battles were fought and its heroes lived and died. There'll always be more you don't know, but that will provide you with an excuse for making yet another visit.

Most Americans in England visit London. Some squeeze in a quick trip to Oxford or Cambridge or Stonehenge. A few rent cars and drive motorways to Scotland or Bath, while those with the time and inclination can drive slowly along miles of bypassed country lanes into the heart of England. But cyclists have it better still: They are *always* on bypassed lanes, and they don't have to stop when paving ends and a sign warns "Unfit for Cars." The cyclist burns no expensive gasoline and makes no fumes; he hardly disturbs cows and sheep and birds at all. He enters the country world quietly; he does it no damage, and for his considerateness he is rewarded by intimate views of what is considered by many to be the most beautiful countryside in the world.

London is a great city—an exciting, stimulating city—but a cosmopolitan one. London is not England. England is stone parish churches; hedgerows with chaffinches, wrens and bluebells; purple heather on open moors; fishing villages on rocky cliffs; flower gardens; dairy farms; sheep runs. Despite its overall population density, rural England is still rural, offering salubrious tranquility to jangled urban nerves, be they British or American. The quiet of rural England is not the quiet of the immense American wilderness; it is the quiet of a vast lived-in park. We once met a Dutchman in the north of England who had driven up from the Channel coast. He was almost unbelieving of what he had seen. "The whole country is like one large garden," he kept repeating.

You don't have to be particularly rugged or aggressively outdoorsy to cycle in England. Distances are short, people are helpful, the terrain is moderate, and the climate equable. With good planning and a judicious use of the excellent rail system, you can have a delightful cycling holiday in England without tackling a single mountain pass—unless you choose to.

What about experienced cyclists who enjoy riding for its own sake, regardless of country? Should they bother loading their bikes on a plane in order to ride in England? We think so.

One reason is the fine road system. England is an old country. New roads have been added over the years while most of the old ones have been maintained. Auto traffic migrates to the newer, wider roads, leaving the old, narrow ones to local traffic, farm vehicles and bicycles. Thus the cyclist can travel almost everywhere on quiet, well-paved roads virtually free of motor traffic.

Also, England's topography lends itself to cycling. You can't ride thirty miles and not be refreshed by variety. In most areas the scene changes quite markedly in a day's ride. There are no vast stretches of a single landscape in England; hills, valleys, mountains and flatlands alternate rapidly—and the coast is never very far away. England is approximately the size of New York State; it could fit almost twice into the state of Oregon. Yet that small area contains most of the topographical variety found in larger countries.

Cycletouring began a long time ago in England. The Cyclists' Touring Club will be a hundred years old in 1978. The experience of an American cyclist isn't complete until he has met old-time British cyclists with years of tradition behind them—and years to have developed amusing eccentricities along with solid, no-frills cycling know-how. A cycletourist should go to England for the same reason a tennis player goes to Wimbledon or a rower to Henley: This is where it all began.

Cycling in rural England is less dangerous than being a pedestrian in almost any big city. People usually have two things in mind when they ask about safety—crime and road safety.

As it has in most western countries, the crime rate in Britain has climbed in recent years. But to an American, it will hardly seem so. The chances of your being hit over the head or knocked off your bike are extremely small. The odds become even greater outside large cities—and a cyclist has no reason to seek out cities. In the countryside you have more chance of hurting yourself in a fall than you do of being hurt by another human being.

What about bicycle thefts? First, insure your bike. Second, be reasonably careful in London and other large cities. If you don't want to worry at all, take a quarter-inch hardened steel welded chain and a good lock with you from home; they're hard to find in England. Among British cyclists, those who bother with a chain at all use bent steel chains, which are about as strong as those used for dog leashes in the States. Even a serious bike thief would be unprepared for a hardened steel chain.

As long as you stay off major roads (those designated with the letter A), there's little likelihood of a serious encounter with a motor vehicle. Occasionally, you'll be confronted by a bus on a lane so narrow that two cyclists could hardly ride next to each other. You and it stop and one squeezes by; the driver is just happy that you're not in a car, in which case you or he would have to back up until you found a passing place.

Some British cyclists, of course, get injured and even killed by vehicles, but those who do, have done two things you won't be doing: They routinely ride on A roads as the fastest way to get to their chosen touring area; and they ride at night. Excessive speed can be dangerous. Some hill and mountain roads are graded very steeply, much more steeply than is usual in the States. Don't be too proud to walk down a hill or around a curve that looks nearly impossible.

From the point of view of physical danger, there is no reason why a man or woman can't ride alone in rural England. The possibility of mishap is not totally absent, but it is much less than the danger a lone woman faces in daytime in most cities. If you ride alone, you forego the assurance of immediate help in case of road accident or mechanical breakdown; you also have to carry a bit more weight since there is no one with whom to split the tools and spare parts. But two women riding together can have all the advantages of any cycling partnership.

Women need not fear being unable to keep up with a group which includes male riders. Riding day after day, women seem to get stronger and, in our experience at least, are actually more durable tourists than men. Even in cycle racing, where pure strength counts for more, you'll find that the top women average only one or two miles an hour slower than the leading men.

In addition to being healthful, relaxing, and harmless to the environment, cycling is inexpensive. If you bring your bike with you from home, the only cost of riding in England will be for wear and tear and replacement of worn parts, probably only a tire, or tube or two. Both depreciation and replacement parts are negligible expenses. If you buy a new bike in England, you'll be paying quite a bit less than you would for the same bike in the States. If you decided to sell a bike you bought in England as soon as you got it home, you would most likely be able to get back what you paid for it. So either way, your transportation costs as a cycletourist will be minimal.

Along with hitchhiking and walking, cycling is the cheapest way to get around. Fares on British Rail average around eight cents a mile; and the more short trips you take, the higher the per mile rate goes. Even at the eight-cent figure, traveling a thousand miles would cost $80. And British Rail can only take you where its track goes. To get anything like the flexibility cycling gives you to get off the beaten track, you'd have to have a car. Currently it costs about $100 per week to rent a small car in England, plus gas. If you drove about a thousand miles over three weeks, the bill would come to about $350. Bicycling will cost almost nothing and give you a better view. Even walking up hills has its compensations; you have time for detailed observation of roadside plants and wildlife, and can pick all the berries you can eat if you travel in late summer or early fall.

While cycling in England, you can eat in expensive restaurants and stay in historic country inns; or you can eat bread and cheese under a tree and sleep in a tent or youth hostel. Obviously, the first sort of tour will cost more than the second.

Let's start with the average costs for staying in bed-and-breakfast places (see p. 81), eating one restaurant meal a day, and having a picnic-style second meal. Bed-and-breakfast should average around £2 ($4.60). A restaurant meal can usually be had for something over a pound; let's assume a £1.40 ($3.20) average. Buying bread, cheese, fruit, etc., in grocery stores will add about 60p ($1.40) to the daily bill. This adds up to about £4, or $9.20, a day. To this must be added extras like train fares, admission charges, cycle parts, laundry, postage, maps, etc. In all, the daily average should be close to $10. Thus for a forty-five day trip, one should allow at least $450 per person. Taking an extra hundred dollars should alleviate worries about running out of money.

Those who want to can cut the $10-a-day average in a number of ways. Foregoing the restaurant meal should save 50p–75p ($1.15–$1.75) a day. Staying in hostels will average about a pound less than staying in bed-and-breakfast places. If you both hostel and skip the restaurant meal, the daily saving comes to about £1.50, leaving your daily expenses at about $6.50. The cycle-camper should cut another fifty cents off this, bringing the cost pretty close to what used to be the magic figure for economy travel in Europe, $5 a day.

We've found it most convenient to carry money in the form of travelers' checks in pounds sterling. That way everyone's happy to cash them, there's no delay while exchange rates are calculated, and you don't have to pay the usual service charge for conversion from a foreign currency. Barclays Bank, or its agents, will convert your dollars to pounds and issue you travelers' checks free of charge.

In general, you can be certain that almost everything connected with cycling will cost less in England. This goes for whole bikes, components and accessories, tools, spare parts and cycling clothing. Unless your vacation is so short that you don't want to waste any time in cycle shops, you can save money and meet some interesting people by planning to buy what you need in Britain.

Two things you should bring from home, however, if you want them, are a good security chain and lock, and lightweight nylon touring bags. Hardened-steel chains and good locks are available in Britain, but you have to search for them. It's easier to bring them from home. Similarly, if you want lightweight touring bags, such as those made by Gerry or Bellwether, you should buy them in the States and bring them with you. English manufacturers specialize in what English cyclists have preferred up to now—somewhat heavier but indestructible black canvas saddle and pannier bags. If you want to try using these, wait and buy Carradice or Karrimor bags in England.

It's difficult to give advice about whether you should bring your bike with you from home or should buy a new one. If you don't own a bike or don't want to tour on the one you have, it pays to purchase a new bike in England. It will cost less there and likely be put together by an experienced bicycle mechanic. Also, picking up a bike in England will let you take the plane from the States without having to worry whether your bike will make it over the Atlantic with you. If you're planning a short tour, however, you can save time by bringing your bike from home.

As long as you don't exceed the regular forty-four pound (twenty kilo) weight limit, you should be able to take your bicycle on transatlantic flights as part of your personal luggage at no extra charge. Taking bikes on such flights is not uncommon, but it hasn't happened frequently enough for standardized policies to have been developed by most airlines. You can check with different airlines to see what their regulations are, if they have any. We've had mostly good luck crossing the Atlantic with bikes three times. Twice they came on the plane with us and had not a spoke bent; the other time they also arrived in perfect condition, but three weeks after we did.

As might be expected, if you travel out of season on an uncrowded plane you're unlikely to have any difficulty. On a packed charter flight an awkwardly shaped, space-consuming bike just might get left behind. Taking a bike apart and putting it in a cardboard box makes a bulky, heavy package—though some airlines will only handle bikes in boxes. We reason that the easier the bike is to handle, the more chance it has of getting on the plane. Therefore, we like to leave it sufficiently intact so it can be wheeled out to the plane. If you try this, you should at least remove the pedals, let some air out of the tires (so they won't explode on decompression), and protect the paint by wrapping newspaper around the frame. It's a good idea also to remove the chain, chainrings and rear derailleur. Removing these parts serves three purposes: It saves them from possible damage; it makes the bike a few pounds lighter; and it removes from sight the parts that most worry airline officials. They have nightmares about damage claims from other passengers whose luggage is punctured by chainrings or ruined forever by dirty grease from a bicycle chain. Brake levers always look particularly vulnerable to damage, so we release the pressure on the brake cable and tie the levers securely to the handlebar with cord.

You're unlikely to be overweight on the plane if you're taking a reasonable load to cycle with. To be able to impress airline personnel with the lightness of your load, should any difficulty arise, you can load your "hand luggage" (a pannier bag) with parts removed from the bike—security chain, power chain, chainrings, derailleur, tools and spare parts. This leaves the bike astonishingly light. If someone objects to your taking a bike as personal luggage, it may help if you know the name of the airline official with whom you checked earlier. Should you have to get into an argument, remember that airlines routinely take skis and golf clubs as personal luggage.

If you are taking a plane to London, try to get one that lands at Gatwick Airport, which has a British Rail station at its front door. This makes it much more convenient for cyclists than Heathrow or other London airports which offer only bus transport into the city. At the moment, only some charter flights land at Gatwick. If you're planning to ride in the north of England or Scotland, it might pay to look into getting a flight to Prestwick, Scotland.

If you take a bike with you from the States, you will have no difficulty on your return if the bike was manufactured here. If, however, it was made abroad, as most good bikes are, you should register it with Customs officials here before you leave. This can be done at Customs offices in large cities or at international airports. If you don't live near a Customs office, you'll have to take care of it at the airport just before you leave. Officials almost always want to see the item being registered, but you might get by with a convincing bill of sale or insurance policy that shows the serial number of the bike as well as the trade name and model. Remember, too, that like any other tourist returning from abroad, you can be charged duty on a Japanese camera, Swiss watch, or any other item of foreign origin, unless you have a registration slip proving you owned it prior to your departure.

If you buy a new bike in Britain, you're in a different position with U.S. Customs. The tariff on twenty-seven-inch lightweight bicycles is currently 5½ percent. Let's suppose your new bike cost $200 and you're bringing it home with you. You're allowed $100 worth of goods duty-free, so if you have nothing else to declare the $100 allowance will be subtracted from the cost of the bike, leaving you to pay 5½ percent on $100. Be prepared to pay the $5.50 and be on your way. From our experience, however, Customs inspectors are much more concerned with drugs than with collecting a few dollars' duty on a bike which is now used and obviously worth less than its original price.

2/The Touring Bike

Some old-timers in England tour on all sorts of odd bikes, but ten- and fifteen-speed lightweight cycles are preferred by most—and with good reason. Such a bike, with carriers, fenders (mudguards) and wired-on (clincher) tires still weighs not more than thirty pounds and is able to carry a load eight or nine times its own weight with ease and safety.

Below is a discussion of the major components of lightweight derailleur-equipped bikes and some points about each to keep in mind when ordering or choosing a touring bike.

Frame. If you are going to spend a disproportionate amount for one part of your bike, make that part the frame. If you want to cut costs, economize on pedals, hubs, rims or cranks; but get the best frame you can. In England the best frames are made with Reynolds

531 manganese-molybdenum alloy steel, single-thickness or double-butted. Single-thickness is a little less expensive; butted tubing, with ends thickened internally where the stress is greatest, is a necessity on racing machines and a worthwhile extra on a touring bike. You should expect Reynolds 531 of some kind on bikes costing about £75 ($170) or more.

A touring frame is not a racing frame. A touring frame is designed to absorb road shock and to give a smooth, stable ride over a variety of surfaces, paved and unpaved. It sacrifices a fraction of efficiency to achieve this end. A racing frame is more rigid and stiff. The racer feels every imperfection of the road surface, but for him this is a small price to pay for increased power and efficiency. As the racing frame hardly bends at all, the rider's every ounce of effort is translated into speed. But because of its rigidity and other factors of design, a frame built for racing is a rather tiring one for a tourist to ride; and sometimes, when carrying a load it was not designed to handle, such a bike can also be unstable.

It's hard to tell a racing frame from a lightweight touring frame merely by looking at the two. The difference may be in a slight variation in the angle between the top tube and the seat tube, say from 72° to 73°; or in a couple of inches difference in overall length; or in the rake (bend) of the fork. In practice, you have to trust the person building or selling the frame to provide you with the right one for your purposes. In England framebuilders make a careful distinction between racing and touring frames, and no one stands to gain by it if you get the wrong sort.

High quality frames are not made in "ladies'" models. For maximum strength with minimum weight, the top tube must be parallel to the ground.

Gearing. After the frame, the most important thing to consider is gearing. The tourist wants low gears to be able to climb as many hills as possible without having to get off and walk. Gears are usually expressed in inches representing the *effective* diameter of the rear wheel. If your rear wheel were ninety inches in diameter instead of twenty-seven your bike would be very hard to pedal, but it would go very fast once you got it moving. Conversely, if the wheel were only twenty inches across, it would be easy to pedal, but no matter how fast your feet spun, you wouldn't move very quickly.

The tourist wants gears down to the low thirty-inch range. Alpine riding makes good use of gears down to the low twenties. A good, all-purpose pair of tourist chainrings, the set of gears attached to the pedal cranks, would be something like a 30-46 or 32-46; this means that the chainrings would have 30 (or 32) and 46 teeth respectively. The smaller chainring gives the lower gears for hill climbing; the larger one is used for riding with the wind on level ground and for downhills. A suitable touring freewheel, the set of gears attached to the rear wheel axle, might be a 14-16-19-23-28. If you wanted to have a very low gear for steep hills, the largest cog could even have 30 or 32 teeth. If the smaller chainring

THE CAMPAGNOLO GRAN TURISMO IS A STRONG, DEPEND-
ABLE WIDE-RANGE (TOURING) REAR DERAILLEUR. THE
NUMBERS ON ITS BODY INDICATE THAT IT CAN HANDLE
CHAINRINGS FROM 36 TO 54 TEETH AND A FREEWHEEL
WITH COGS OF 13 TO 36 TEETH.

and the largest cog on the freewheel have the same number of teeth, you have a low gear of twenty-seven inches, the true diameter of the rear wheel. (See Appendix F for a complete gear chart.)

Not all rear derailleurs (gear changers) can handle the wide range of cog sizes and gears desired by the cycletourist. A wide-range derailleur is usually called for. In Europe two of the best touring derailleurs are made by Campagnolo. The new Rally model is highly praised and very expensive; the Gran Turismo is tough, reliable and more moderately priced. Japanese components have been slow to appear in England, but if you can find them the Shimano Crane GS and Sun Tour VGT are first-rate rear changers.

Hubs, rims and spokes. High-flange (racing-style) hubs are seen on most bikes imported into the United States, but low-flange hubs, with their longer spokes, allow the wheel a bit more flexibility and give a more comfortable ride. Thus low-flange types are chosen by most European cycletourists, and even by racers when running over rough ground. Quick-release hubs are for racers, who have to change wheels in seconds; They're not needed for touring.

Rims are made of steel or aluminum. Steel is stronger and stands up better to rugged off-the-road use; also steel rims can be hammered back into shape if they do get knocked out of round. Aluminum rims are more expensive, lighter, more carefully machined and they don't rust. But their lack of strength may be a problem, especially for the cyclist who has a

QUICK-RELEASE SKEWERS AND HIGH-FLANGE HUBS ARE FOUND ON RACING BIKES—AND BIKES TRYING TO LOOK "RACEY." (top) LOW-FLANGE HUBS SECURED BY HEX NUTS ARE LESS "FLASHY," (bottom) BUT THEY ARE PERFECTLY SERVICEABLE FOR TOURING. ACTUALLY, THE SMALL FLANGE ALLOWS FOR A LONGER SPOKE AND THUS FOR A MORE COMFORTABLE RIDE.

heavy load or who occasionally leaves paved roads. Consider the kind of riding you plan to do and your weight and luggage load when choosing between aluminum and steel.

Most lightweight bikes come with 36 spokes in both front and rear wheels, but British tourists usually choose a rear wheel with 40 spokes for added strength where most of the load is. In front they often drop to 32 spokes. Having 40 in back is a very good idea; either 32 or 36 is fine in front.

There are butted spokes and single-gauge ones; the butted save weight for racers, but single-gauge are generally stronger for tourists.

Tires and pumps. Most tourists prefer wired-on, or clincher, tires. These have a separate tire and tube and thus are easy to patch. They are also stronger and more resistant to cuts than are racing-style tubular, or sew-up, tires. If you decide on wired-on tires, you'll find that in Britain they come with either Schraeder or Presta valves. Presta valves have been standard there but are slowly being phased out in favor of Schraeder valves, which are standard in the United States. We prefer the Presta because the valve has no spring and therefore nothing to wear out. Since each type of valve requires a different size hole drilled through the rim, you cannot change from one to the other easily. Whichever valve you choose, always remember to ask for spare tubes of the same type and make sure your pump fits it.

A good pump is an absolute necessity. You cannot

fill your tires at gas stations. Your tires will get only as much air in them as you and your pump can force there. Many pumps will not get high-pressure tires sufficiently hard. Some pumps that use a flexible connector to attach to the tube's valve will not be satisfactory—though the Bluemels usually works well. The best pumps have a head with a rubber gasket which fits directly over the valve and has to be knocked off; it doesn't screw on. Once you get the knack of using it, a pump of this type, such as the Silca, will deliver as much pressure as you want. It costs about $8 in England and comes in various lengths to match your bike's seat-tube length, so no extra hardware is needed to carry it.

Brakes. Center-pull brakes are best. Mafac and Weinmann have good reputations. With the extra weight of touring gear, it will take 10 to 20 percent longer to stop, and even 100 percent or more when the brakes are wet. If there is room to mount them, you can get increased braking power with extra-long brake blocks, the kind usually seen on tandems.

Fenders and saddle. Fenders (mudguards) are a necessity. You cannot ride day after day, in all kinds of weather, without full mudguards. Good, light plastic ones are made by Bluemels and Bantel.

Exposure to all kinds of weather and to overnight rain and dew is rough treatment for a leather saddle. If you must use one, treat the top and underside with a waterproofing wax, and try to cover it at night.

To save the trouble, we leave the leather saddles at home and tour on all plastic ones. They're almost as comfortable and are indifferent to weather.

Toe clips, lights and cyclometer. Toe clips are a must. If you aren't used to them, start with the straps loose and tighten them over a few days as you get to feel more comfortable. It's much easier to ride when your foot is held in its proper position on the pedal, and being able to pull up as well as to push down increases your efficiency considerably.

There's not much reason for a foreign tourist to ride at night; it's hardly the way to see a country. One of those small, battery-operated French arm lights is useful to have along for emergencies. If you do think you might want to do some night riding, or just want to be prepared, visit a cycle shop in England and get fitted out with lights that meet government standards. A front white light as well as a rear red light and reflector are required by law for nighttime riding. The red light must have the British Standard marking "B.S. 3648."

A cyclometer is a useful accessory. Apart from satisfying curiosity about how far you've ridden, being aware of your exact mileage aids in pinpointing your position on a map.

Tandems. A large number of people planning to take their first extended cycletour with a companion consider riding a tandem. Usually this is a mistake. Riding a tandem successfully takes a coordination of strength, temperament and riding style of which many experienced cyclists are incapable, and which is almost certainly beyond the skill of beginners. Also, the rider in back always has his view limited by his partner in front; nor does the rear rider get to steer, change gears or brake. Because of its size and weight, a tandem always requires two people, so it's impossible for one partner to take an evening ride or a short trip without the other. In addition, a tandem is harder to manipulate on and off trains and planes, and it has much less room for carrying bags than two single bikes would have. You still have only two wheels with a luggage carrier over each.

Nonetheless, many people have been riding tandems happily for years. If you enjoy teamwork and absolute togetherness, a tandem might be for you. The weight of one tandem is less than two single cycles and wind resistance is almost halved, often allowing a tandem team to easily outdistance single riders of equal strength. And tandems are useful for older riders and people with various physical handicaps. Many who could not handle their own bikes, such as blind people, make good use of them.

The preceding discussion of bicycle types and parts is intended as a guide for prospective buyers. But there are no absolute "requirements" for cycletouring. Clearly, you can have a great time riding a bike which doesn't even approximate the ideal touring bike.

If you are thinking seriously of buying a new bike in England, get in correspondence with a couple of cycle shops or frame builders as far in advance as possible. Whether you want an inexpensive factory-made bike or a custom-built frame, write early. A year in advance is not too soon, especially if you want a bike built for you from the frame up. Some custom frame builders are taking orders two and three years in advance, but usually orders for bikes which are being picked up in person can be squeezed in.

When you write, state prices in pounds sterling. Some people are unfamiliar with United States currency, and all will be wary of committing themselves to a price in a foreign currency in these times of fluctuating exchange rates. In your letter you can describe the kind of bike you want and ask what it will cost. Or, if you're not certain about exactly what you want, you can state how much you want to spend and ask the dealer what sort of touring bike he can give you for the money. If you do this with a few dealers you can "comparison shop" across the Atlantic.

With your initial letter include an International Reply Coupon, and politely request a reply by air mail. If you don't do this, you'll be astonished how many answers will arrive by sea mail, stained and rumpled, two months later. International Reply Coupons are on sale at all post offices.

Even if you want to buy only a relatively inexpensive cycle, in the $100 to $150 price range, it pays to order in advance. The English are much more economical than Americans about some things, and one of them is space in cycle shops; even well-known stores like Holdsworth and Ron Kitching are quite small by our standards. They don't have space to stock and display large number of assembled bikes. Many shops have no finished bikes on display at all; they have a few frames hanging from the ceiling and components stocked on shelves like an old-fashioned hardware store. This way of doing business generally works to the buyer's advantage, but you can seldom go into a shop, buy a ready-to-go bike, and ride out the door.

If you want to spend less than about £65 ($150), you will probably have to choose among factory-built cycles, such as one of the less expensive Raleigh ten-speed models. In this price range the only reason to write in advance is to allow the dealer time to order from the factory and have the bike ready for you. He will make minor changes which you request, such as substituting a different derailleur or adding luggage carriers, but basically you'll be getting the bike as it was when it left the factory.

Once you spend more than about $150, you can get a bike which, to a greater or lesser extent, has been chosen and assembled with your specific cycling needs in mind. If you are spending this much, it is not advisable to merely order a factory-made bike; at every price level but the lowest you'll get more for your money by having a small cycle shop put your bike together.

Suppose you want to spend from £65 to £80 ($150 to $185). What will you be getting? The frame of the bike will not be custom-made; it will be one of those that were hanging from the ceiling. You should get to choose the color. The frame's three main tubes, at least, should be made of Reynolds 531. You will indicate that you want a touring frame and choose the size, in inches. If you aren't sure what frame size to select, tell the dealer your height and inside leg measurement from crotch to heel standing barefoot.

In this moderate price range you cannot specify details about every part of the bike. You should indicate your preferences in some important parts, but you have to leave the rest to the judgment of the dealer. You will want to be certain you have low gears and a wide-range derailleur; you could even ask for a specific model such as the Gran Turismo, but you shouldn't also insist on a specific make of chain, saddle or pedal.

You don't necessarily have to have a bike built from the frame up to get a good touring bike. A few companies build a bike especially for touring and sell it as a completed unit—all you do is choose the frame size. One such bike is made by Holdsworth and another by Bob Jackson. (See Appendix D for addresses.) The Holdsworth is a good value at about £115 ($260). It has alloy cranks, mudguards and carrier already fitted, and uses some Campagnolo parts, including the Rally rear derailleur.

From somewhere around £100 and up you can get a frame custom-built for you and fitted with most or all of the components of your choice. Some of the better-known sellers of hand-built British frames are Condor, Holdsworth and Witcomb in the London area, and in the Midlands and north Bob Jackson, Jack Taylor, Ron Kitching and R.E.W. Reynolds. There are also many small frame-builders in England who aren't widely known because they produce only a few frames a month, but whose products are generally excellent. Sometimes you will order a frame by size; other builders may want to know your leg and arm measurements and weight. If you have the money and do enough cycling to make it pay off, a finely crafted frame is worth every dollar it costs. It will be built with Reynolds 531 double-butted tubing and have hand-filed lugs, usually with details outlined in a contrasting color.

While we'd encourage any serious cyclist with the cash to order a custom frame, once the tourist spends over about £130 ($300) he gets less return for each additional dollar spent. Above that price most of the added refinements save ounces, or fractions thereof, for the racer, but are only marginally useful for the tourist. If you throw a pound loaf of bread in your bag, you negate the weight-saving bought by $100 worth of lightweight alloy parts. There's little reason for a touring bike to be fitted with expensive Campagnolo brakes, hubs, pedals, cranks, seatpost and headset. If you must have the very best, and money is no object, go ahead and buy it, but you should know that your bike will be only slightly lighter than one costing much less.

As a rule, one shouldn't count on finding a good used bike suitable for touring in a few days of shopping around in England. You'd expect to have trouble in the States finding a used bike that fits you, has the gearing you want, a suitable frame and no worn or damaged parts; and the chances of discovering your dream bike for sale at half its worth are no better in England. There just aren't that many serious cyclists in the whole country, and most of them keep their bikes a long, long time—and then give them to a friend. Most bikes in ordinary use are heavy three-speed models not suitable for touring.

If, however, you will be in England for a while before you want to start cycling, you could look around at different cycle shops and read advertisements. Occasionally a good used touring bike comes up for sale in the small ads sections of *Cycletouring*, the magazine of the Cyclists' Touring Club. Though you ought to start off reconciled to the idea of purchasing a new bike, you might be lucky in finding a used one. It does happen. We know someone who got a Holdsworth cycle at a bike shop in Oxford for $50. It was designed for racing and isn't completely suitable for touring; still, it's a beautiful machine worth three or four times its price.

Apart from getting on the mailing list for *Cycletouring*, there are other reasons, some sentimental some practical, to join the Cyclists' Touring Club (CTC). The club is the oldest such organization in the world. It began in 1878 and provided the model for cycling clubs on the Continent, and for the

League of American Wheelmen here. Later motoring clubs, the Automobile Association (AA) in Britain and our American Automobile Association (AAA), were also patterned after the CTC.

Most of the articles in *Cycletouring* are devoted to touring in Britain, and even the ads are of interest—you get an idea of the equipment favored by British cyclists and what it costs. Other practical benefits of club membership include: free legal aid if you're involved in a road accident in the United Kingdom; third-party insurance up to £250,000 good anywhere in the world; the CTC *Handbook*, a concise source of information on ferry services, accommodations, cycle repairers and much more; information sheets on touring in Britain and on the Continent; and access to CTC local information officers throughout the British Isles. In addition, you can purchase any of the Bartholomew half-inch (or metric 1:100,000) maps and selected Ordnance Survey maps through the club at a discount. This service is available by mail; allow two months for delivery of maps by sea mail. You can also purchase insurance for yourself and your cycle through the CTC.

The club's major annual get-together, the York Rally, takes place early each July on the Knavesmire, a racetrack just outside the city of York. Some Americans plan their riding so they can take in the Rally. It's a two-day weekend affair with a program of cycling-related events, races, etc., and a large display of their latest wares by frame-builders, component manufacturers, clothiers and shoemakers. For

RIDERS OF ALL AGES GATHER FOR THE GRAND PARADE
AT THE CYCLISTS' TOURING CLUB'S YORK RALLY.

a nominal fee you can pitch your tent at the racetrack; or you can stay in York and cycle the two or
three miles to the Knavesmire.

Adult membership in the CTC costs £3.70 ($9.25);
junior membership, for those under eighteen, costs
£1.80 ($4.50). Send a check in dollars, or, prefer-
ably, an International Money Order in pounds
sterling, with your name and address to: The Secre-
tary, CTC, Cotterell House, 69 Meadrow, Godalming,
Surrey, England. If you want only to subscribe to
Cycletouring send a check for $3.75 to the same ad-
dress.

3/Planning Ahead

If at all possible, plan your trip to England for some time other than the last week or two in July or the first half of August. Some time around July 20th *everyone* seems to go on vacation. Many factories close then and schools begin a six-week holiday. Monumental traffic jams develop at the strangest hours as Englishmen start midnight excursions to the Channel coast, the southwest, Wales, the Lake District, Scotland and car-ferry ports east, south and west. In the middle of the summer you'll find obscure and even unattractive bed-and-breakfast places booked full in advance.

If weather be your guide, you should know that statistically you have the least chance of being rained on in June, and the most chance in October and November. But it's useful to keep in mind that geography is more significant than the calendar in determining your chances of getting dry weather. In all months, the eastern, lowland, and some would say less interesting, side of Britain is drier than the hilly and mountainous western side. Besides, statistics have only a statistical validity; a couple of years ago we enjoyed a bright, colorful, warm October with hardly a drop of rain.

Few will argue against May, the second driest month, and June, the driest, as being ideal for a cycling vacation in England. Who can say anything against an English spring? Resorts are open but still uncrowded, wildflowers and cottage gardens are in bloom, skylarks are singing, and bed-and-breakfast operators are still unjaded.

What about avoiding the tourist season altogether and traveling in winter? Climate isn't too much against you. It rarely gets colder than 35°–40°F, and snow amounting to anything generally only falls in the hills and in the north. Roads and places of interest will be uncrowded, although some tourist attractions will be closed in the off-season. Many places in England offer reduced rates in the winter, as do the airlines. You and your bike will be looked on with kindly curiosity, and you'll have little trouble with airline baggage clerks, British Rail conductors and ferry operators. In our experience, the best thing about cycling in winter is that everyone seems to be more relaxed and to have more time for you. In tiny villages you may even become a legend overnight—the cyclist who came in one dusky November afternoon and left in that terrible rain the next morning when it was barely light. The English will admire you; they reserve their highest respect for someone who seems to have chosen the hardest course voluntarily.

Most of the disadvantages of winter cycling are obvious. Chilly, wet weather can eventually dampen the warmest enthusiasm. With proper clothing you can almost always keep warm while riding; we've found the worst cold comes in the long, dark afternoons and nights in unheated houses. Some nights we wore down jackets, which have kept us warm through upstate New York winters, to no avail. (Don't worry about hurting anyone's feelings by wearing your outdoor jacket in the house; in rural places, especially in Ireland, it's accepted.)

Two final considerations in planning a winter tour: In areas where the major industry is tourism, most places will be closed completely during the off-season; this is especially true of coastal resorts whose main attraction is sea-bathing. The other thing to consider is that northern Europe is very far north indeed, and the days grow very short when you reach December. There's reasonable light for winter riding only from about 9:00 A.M. to 3:30 P.M. Fitting your bike with good lights might be a reasonable precaution for a winter tour. Because of the shortness of the day and the increased chance for snowy weather, one should not plan to cycle in northern England or Scotland during the winter months.

The good side of long, cold nights is that you'll get to spend many of them chatting before a warm fire, either where you're staying or in the pub down the road. Also you'll do a lot more reading and letter writing than in the summer when it's light until 10:00 P.M. and you just can't bring yourself to go inside.

There is no getting around the fact that the more you know about England before you leave home, the more you'll get out of your trip. It's easy to begin gathering information—there's certainly been more written about England than any other similarly sized piece of real estate on earth. You can start by contacting the British Tourist Authority, with offices in New York City, Chicago and Los Angeles. (See Appendix B for addresses.) Stop in or write, giving them some idea what sort of information you want. From the literature you receive you'll discover new sources of information to which you can write for further details about your particular interests (aside from cycling), be they architecture, birds, caves, gliding, narrow-gauge railways, canals, farming, geology—whatever.

Once you start receiving pamphlets and maps of England in the mail, you'll begin to feel yourself already closer to the other side of the Atlantic. But don't forget about other sources of information, like the local library. It's impossible to begin to suggest what books are worth reading; there are far too many of them, and individual tastes and interests differ. But whatever your interests, you should be able to find books about them in your local library.

One general point about selecting books: Don't

assume a book has to be new to be useful. Old accounts of travels are often even more fascinating; sometimes you can do some exciting detective work trying to see what's changed in the last one or two hundred years. Americans might want to look into the observations on travel in England by such nineteenth-century countrymen as Washington Irving, Nathaniel Hawthorne, Ralph Waldo Emerson and Henry James. Don't overlook old guidebooks, either on library shelves or in secondhand bookstores. Also, many eighteenth-century English novels are fun to read and give you a picture of a world you'll still recognize widely in rural England. Novels to start with might include *Humphrey Clinker* and *Tom Jones*. Earlier still, Daniel Defoe wrote a guide to Britain that's available in a modern edition; while from the early nineteenth century come the incomparable novels of Jane Austen. Whatever and however much you read, you'll wish you had read more once you get to England.

Rather than add the weight of this book or any other to your cycling load, it might be wiser to take brief notes to carry along. We did this before our last trip, arranged them by county in the order we would be traveling, and carried them in a small waterproof binder. This takes up almost no room and adds very little weight, yet holds a lot of information reminding you to look for things you might otherwise miss.

As you read you might also use a map of England as a bookmark, putting a dot on the map at places you think you want to see. After weeks or months of doing this, a pattern may emerge. Maybe your dots will congregate in Wiltshire or Yorkshire or the Cotswolds. Then it might be time to order Bartholomew maps for those areas. (See Appendix C for addresses.) Once you have your maps, you can begin to think about specific routes. You'll discover that places which seemed close are separated by hills, and others which seemed far apart are separated by an easy ride down a river valley. If you plan to hostel, this is the time to begin to pay some attention to their locations; these are marked on the Bartholomew maps. But it is *not* necessary to plan where you will stay each night. This kind of detailed itinerary may be necessary in remote sections, like the Scottish Highlands, but England is a small country with accommodations so easy to find that you can almost always enjoy the flexibility of getting up in the morning, seeing how you feel, looking at the sky, and then deciding how far to ride that day. You may even change your plans midday should you stop at points of interest along the way and find you want to spend more time sightseeing than you had planned. Learn all you can about the things you want to see along your route, but don't ride your bike as if it were a railway train forced to keep to the tracks and an assigned schedule.

Put out of your mind an itinerary based on the "challenge" of geography alone. Let your interests, not geography, determine your route.

Suppose you decide to spend a week in the Salisbury Plain area and a week in the Cotswolds. You could start in the Cotswolds by taking the train from London to Oxford and then work your way south to Salisbury Plain, perhaps ending your tour in Winchester and taking the train from there back to London. If you wanted to ride in Devon and Cornwall, you could take the train to Exeter. There you'd be only a couple of miles from Dartmoor and about thirty miles, over the moor, from the Cornwall border. Similarly, if you wanted to ride in Yorkshire or the Lake District, you could start by taking the train to York or Kendal or Carlisle. If you want to spend a week or two touring in each of widely separated areas, such as the Cotswolds and the Lake District, take British Rail from one to the other.

You'll get the most out of your trip and the miles you ride if you control the impulse to merely pile up mileage. It's much better to get to know a small area well than to ride seventy-five miles a day superficially over the face of the land. To make the most of your time, take the train to where you really want to ride. No matter how much time you have, you can use it best if you think of your tour as being divided into a series of separate cycling trips linked by journeys via British Rail. Don't let a foolish consistency convince you there is something ignoble about putting your bike on a train. And don't try to cycle out of London. Even if you plan to ride in the Home Counties, take a train to at least twenty miles from Trafalgar Square.

Taking a bicycle on British Rail presents no problems. Almost all trains, except for local commuter services, are equipped with baggage cars—which, in our experience, are generally uncrowded. You simply wheel your bike to the baggage car, load it aboard yourself and secure it with chain, elastic luggage straps, rope or whatever, so that it won't fall over. On a short trip it is often best to simply stay in the baggage car yourself for the duration of the ride. On a longer trip you can tie the bike securely and then find a seat in a passenger car. It's advisable to return to the baggage car several minutes before you reach your destination so that you will be prepared to wheel your bike off the train as soon as you reach your stop. The bike and the contents of panniers should be quite safe when left in the baggage car, though it might be wise to keep your money and passport in your pocket.

Cyclists not having the time to do all the planning necessary, or who, for whatever reason, don't want to go it alone, might want to ride in England as part of an organized group. The British Cyclists' Touring Club organizes tours of Britain and the Continent from April through September. Schedules and booking information are included in the December/January issue of the club's magazine, *Cycletouring*. Most tours last about two weeks and make extensive use of youth hostels and other inexpensive accommodations. Naturally, on CTC tours most of your fellow cyclists will be Britishers, who should be informative companions in their own land.

On this side of the Atlantic, the American Youth

Hostels (AYH) and the International Bicycle Touring Society (IBTS) regularly organize tours in Britain. (See Appendix A for addresses.) The AYH tours use youth hostel accommodations and thus are close to being as inexpensive as possible. Rooms are dormitory-style, usually with from four to twelve beds. Hostelers tend to be on the younger side of middle age, but there are no age limits and many old-time cyclists and walkers use hostels. The IBTS tours in a more comfortable style. Rooms are booked at inns

THE RIVER ITCHEN WAS ONE OF ISAAC WALTON'S FAVORITE FISHING SPOTS. THIS PICTURE WAS TAKEN FROM THE WINCHESTER YOUTH HOSTEL WHICH OCCUPIES AN OLD MILL SPANNING THE RIVER.

and meals are eaten in restaurants. Baggage is carried in a following station wagon or van, while unencumbered riders pedal lightly down the road. This method of cycletouring particularly appeals to older riders, but younger people are welcome also.

Whether planning to ride alone, with a friend or in a group, a beginning cyclist or one who has not ridden regularly should ideally allow at least a month before starting a tour for getting in shape. If you can't take your practice runs carrying some of the gear you'll be touring with, you can simulate the effort needed to pedal with extra weight by riding in higher gears than you would use normally—but don't begin doing this until you've had at least a week or so in the saddle. It's prudent to assume that the distance you can comfortably ride in a day around home will be cut somewhat when touring. The extra weight of touring gear, the unpredictability of weather, and eating and sleeping more irregularly cut down cycling efficiency.

Once you decide when to cycle in England and for how long, you'll have to decide exactly what to bring with you. Choice of wearing apparel of course depends on season, although, since extremes of temperature are rare in England, you won't need very heavy clothes in the winter or want to be without warm items in the spring and summer.

A down jacket, the kind that fits into a small stuff sack, is recommended for fall and winter, although we also made good use of one on chilly evenings in May and early June. You'll always need a good medium-weight sweater, no matter what the season. We suggest taking a second pair of pants to change into (women might alternate with a pair of culottes) and two or three shirts or tops of some sort. If you choose ones made with synthetic fibers, or synthetic-natural fiber blends, they'll dry quickly. Shorts can be useful for the few hot days you might encounter in the summer, but short-sleeve tops are less necessary. It's better to have loose garments with long sleeves that can be rolled up. Both sexes will find good use for a couple of cotton T-shirts, as they add warmth in cool weather and keep you drier in warm. They're almost a necessity if you're wearing synthetics. It's a good idea to choose your clothes so they can be removed or added layer by layer according to temperature.

A woman should have a skirt along, although culottes are sufficient and are very comfortable for riding in warm weather—better than shorts. A pair of tights comes in handy to use as stockings when you feel the need to be a bit dressed up. They can also be worn for warmth, but shouldn't be worn when riding as they cling and constrict movement.

Gloves are a necessity in most seasons. Medium-weight ski gloves are a good choice for winter cycling. Spring and summer, cycling gloves are recommended; they add comfort and a little warmth on cool days.

For rain nothing is perfect. Capes are open and therefore don't encourage condensation, but they also don't protect you from water splashed up from the road. Also, on those not unusual days when rain

MOUNTAIN ROADS ARE OFTEN NARROW, BUT MOSTLY
TRAFFIC-FREE. THE ROAD PICTURED IS ON THE DINGLE
PENINSULA, CO. KERRY, WESTERN IRELAND, WHERE A
RAINSUIT OFTEN COMES IN HANDY.

is accompanied by wind they make you feel like a
sailboat without a rudder. We have found bright
orange rainsuits made for sailing most effective, but
by no means perfect. Perspiration builds up inside
them so they often end up as wet inside as out. Of
late, the Peter Storm Company has been advertising
a rainsuit that keeps rain out while allowing perspiration to escape. We haven't tried it, so we can't say if
it works as advertised or not. Most Peter Storm products are less expensive in England.

There are public laundromats in cities, towns and even some villages. Riding in remote areas you might not come upon them frequently, but rarely in a week's riding will you not find at least one. If you want to ask directions, ask for the "launderette." Washing and drying one small load costs about $1.50. You can save on laundry bills by using synthetics for much of your wardrobe. These can be washed in a sink and dried overnight in your room.

In a normal day of cycletouring, you'll do plenty of walking as well as riding. Careful selection is required to find shoes suitable for both. Good cycling shoes are lightweight, with thin but stiff soles to protect your feet from the metal pedals; walking shoes are generally heavier and wider, with thick soles and heels.

Most British cycletourists wear shoes specially made for cycling. The touring models are heavier than racing shoes and have raised heels for easier walking. Usually the uppers are not perforated. They are light enough for easy pedaling and shaped to fit into toe clips. If you want to buy cycling shoes designed for touring, wait and get them in England. Almost all the cycling shoes one sees in America are intended for racers. Holdsworth in London has a good selection of shoes. (See Appendix D for address.)

If you want to improvise your footwear, remember that your shoes will have to fit into toe clips. Also you'll want a stiff sole to spread the load between your foot and the edges of the metal pedals. Shoes should not restrict ankle movement; if they do, your cycling efficiency will be diminished.

If you can manage it, carrying a second pair of shoes is recommended. When your cycling shoes get soaked you'll appreciate having a dry pair to change into. Also, when you stop cycling for the day, it's relaxing to have a different pair of shoes to wear. A spare pair of shoes should be light and compact, but they should be sturdy enough for walking and sight-seeing, and for some cycling when necessary. Sandals are useless: You can't cycle in them, they're not good for walking, and they give no protection against nighttime cold.

With allowances for adding or subtracting certain items of clothing according to season, sex and length of stay, the following checklist can serve as a guide for prospective cycletourists. It is based on the items we carried on a three-month spring and summer tour using bed-and-breakfast accommodations. Two cyclists can share most items other than clothing. An unaccompanied cyclist might have to trim the list a bit to keep things manageable.

Clothing

3 or 4 sets of underwear
2 or 3 shirts or tops
2 pair jeans, or 1 jeans, 1 shorts
skirt or culottes
sweater
3 or 4 pair socks

pajamas
slippers or thongs
handkerchiefs
knotted tie
down jacket and stuff sack
windbreaker or shell
hat, cap or head scarf
rainsuit
cycling gloves
cycling shoes
spare shoes

Toilet articles

shampoo
toothbrush and paste
1 towel
soap
small camping mirror
razor and blades
comb and brush
nail clipper
small scissors
pills, medication

Tools, spare parts, etc.

small screw driver
6-inch adjustable wrench
dumbbell wrench
tire irons
chain rivet remover

freewheel remover
cone wrench
spoke wrench
narrow wrench to remove pedals   (*must fit space be-
        tween pedal and crank*)
6 extra spokes
spare front and rear derailleur cables
spare front and rear brake cables
spare nuts, bolts, lockwashers
tire patch kit
tire pump
oil
spare inner tube   (*for clincher tires*)
battery arm light
security chain and lock
talcum powder
plastic electrical tape   (*useful for various emergen-
        cies*)
water bottle
elastic luggage straps
rags

Miscellaneous

glasses
sunglasses
pants-leg ties
wristwatch
camper knife, fork, spoon set
pocket knife
can opener/corkscrew

safety pins
cotton
string
rubber bands
masking tape
plastic bags   (*useful for keeping camera and film dry; for carrying food, wet or dirty clothes; and lots more*)
inflatable hangers
sewing kit
first-aid kit
leather waterproofing wax
dog spray
detergent packets
pens and notebook
maps
alarm clock
camera and film
transistor radio   (*an ordinary AM radio will receive BBC programs, weather reports, etc.*)
compass   (*useful in cities as well as country*)
small binoculars   (*6-power binoculars weight as little as 5.5 oz.*)

4/*Getting Under Way*

The days of leisurely transatlantic crossings are over. Almost everyone who makes the journey now has to fly, which nine times out of ten means leaving the United States in the evening, losing five to eight hours in transit, and landing bleary-eyed and rubber-legged in England the next morning—local time. After this ordeal, you are hardly able to find the exit, much less start cycling.

Rest and time are the only cures for jet fatigue. It takes at least three days for the body to adjust to such an unnatural skipping through time zones. If you brought your bike with you on the plane, you'd be wise to check it at the left-luggage office and forget about it for a few days. If you've landed at Gatwick Airport, you can take a forty-minute ride on British Rail to Victoria Station in London; from Heathrow Airport you must take a bus—at least until the new underground extension is completed, some time in 1977. An alternative might be to stay at a hotel at the airport. They are expensive, but perhaps worth it for one or two nights.

If you're picking up a new bike in England, after a good sleep you ought to write or call the cycle shop where you ordered your bike telling them that you've arrived and will be around to pick it up. If you're in London and your bike is in, say, Leeds, it's as good to write as to telephone. Even within the London area, a letter is often as good as a phone call, as same-day delivery is often possible and many Englishmen seem to regard the telephone as a nasty device which intrudes on people's privacy.

Every cycle, no matter how carefully built, will need last-minute adjustments. If you have the time it would be a good idea to plan a visit to inspect your new bike a day or two before you actually want to start riding. Similarly, if you've brought your bike from home, you should inspect it carefully as you reassemble it to make sure nothing is loose or out of line. Spokes, rims and brakes are the most vulnerable parts; also, if you didn't remove it for the flight, you should check for a bent rear derailleur.

When everything is in order, it's time to load your gear on the bike and be off. The one place you should never carry weight when cycling is in a pack on your back. Weight can be supported by luggage carriers placed over the front or rear wheels, or both. If you have carriers over both wheels, you should never load the front one by itself. Weight added exclusively in front makes steering very difficult. Most British cyclists follow the opposite procedure; they carry the load over the rear wheel and put little or nothing in front. The advantage of this arrangement is that the steering is unaffected by the added weight. You can still turn with little effort and can make quick moves around holes or pieces of glass. The typical British cyclist will tour with a big black canvas saddlebag strapped to the saddle and secured to the seatpost or rear carrier. If more carrying space is needed, a pair of pannier bags is added, also over the rear wheel. If you want to try this arrangement, make sure your rear wheel has forty spokes to help carry the heavy load in back.

We prefer a more equal distribution of weight between the front of the bike and the back. Pairs of pannier bags, front and rear, work well. The panniers get the weight low, so it affects the bike's balance less than the same weight carried in a saddle and handlebar bag combination. In addition, the tops of the carriers are left empty, so light, bulky items like a down jacket or a sleeping bag or food can be strapped on easily. In this system heavier items should always be packed in the rear panniers; the front ones must be lighter. Even with a minimum of weight in the front panniers, you lose some mobility. The advantage of putting some weight in front is that overall the bike is steadier and more stable, especially in wind and on rough roads.

While loading your bags, keep in mind that the postal service can be used to advantage in carrying certain of your goods from one point to another. Suppose you want to tour in two separate areas; two weeks in the southwest and two weeks in Yorkshire. You buy all your maps before you start, then discover that you have nine maps which you'd rather not carry all at once in your bags. If you're starting in the south you can wrap your Yorkshire maps and mail them to yourself at a convenient post office

ONE WAY TO CARRY TOURING GEAR IS IN FRONT AND REAR PANNIER BAGS. THIS LEAVES THE CARRIER TOPS FREE FOR MORE BULKY ITEMS.

where you can pick them up later when you need them. The post office will hold Poste Restante (general delivery) mail for a month.

You may encounter a similar problem with guidebooks and pamphlets which you accumulate along the way. Many of these excellent quality publications are worth saving. These can be collected and mailed home to the States when you move on to a new region.

When mailing maps, books, guides or other printed matter, whether to another part of the United Kingdom or to the States, be sure to take advantage of the low rates available for such packages. To do this, wrap the package so that one end is open and the clerk can see it contains only printed material; tie securely with string. Write in the upper left-hand corner of the addressed side, "Printed Papers—Reduced Rate." This rate will let you mail a two-pound package to the States for about 35¢, and a four-pound package for about 65¢. The rate within the United Kingdom is even lower.

Two other postal bargains are for aerograms and small packets. Aerograms cost 10½ p (24¢); they're the cheapest way to send a letter by air across the Atlantic. Ask about the regulations for small packets. It's a cheap rate for packages of two pounds or less meeting certain qualifications. Once a package weighs more than two pounds, you're into the parcel rate which has the same charge (a high one) for all packages under seven pounds. Postal rates change. To get the best deal, ask at a post office in England;

you should be able to obtain a leaflet there detailing the various rates.

To get mail from the States while you're traveling, you can use Poste Restante. To be on the safe side, figure out where you'll be two weeks from the time you write (air mail, of course), and have your correspondent write to you in care of Poste Restante in that city or town. The address should read: your name, c/o Poste Restante, city, county, England. For example, John Smith, c/o Poste Restante, Tavistock, Devon, England. When you get to a town where you expect mail, simply go to the main post office, show your passport, and ask if they have any mail for you. The service is free.

If, after a week of riding, you discover that you brought too many shirts or you decide to buy a pair of new cycling shoes, you don't have to throw anything away; just make a package and mail it home. To get it through Customs easily, mark the package, "U.S. goods being returned—no commercial value." Similarly, if you see something for sale that you want, don't worry about not being able to carry it; have it wrapped and head for the nearest post office. Three or four pounds of wool yarn is impossibly bulky to carry on a bike; but we've been able to buy comparatively inexpensive yarn of excellent quality in both England and Ireland by using the mail service.

Adding twenty pounds of dead weight almost doubles the weight of a good bicycle and makes it handle quite differently. The most obvious difference

is that it's harder to pedal. You will find
using lower gears more and shifting down so
you begin to ascend hills. But remember that th
will also have more momentum and be harder t
once you get it going. You'll be pulling the k
harder, and an old brake cable is more likely to

Other changes in riding characteristics will
from bike to bike according to its design and
exact amount of weight added where. Generally
loaded bike wants to go straighter than the same b.
free of extra weight. You have to lean more to t
side on turns to ease the front wheel around. If the
is weight in front, turning will take more effor
Whatever surprises your loaded bike has in store fo
you, learn what they are and what you can do to
compensate for them. If you can, ride your fully
loaded bike around home for a few days. If this isn't
possible, plan short rides for the first couple of days
of your tour, until you get used to the added weight.

The change from riding on the right to riding on
the left may be a little harder for an experienced
cyclist to get used to than it is for a beginner, but
it isn't very hard for anyone. If you've not ridden
much in the United States, you'll take naturally to
riding on the left; the only problem will come in
breaking the habit on returning to this country.
Chance for error comes mostly on turns; if there's
no traffic on the street into which you are turning,
you may align yourself instinctively on the right.
Remind yourself to keep left. The left turn is now
the easy one; the right turn requires crossing traffic.

If our traffic laws were designed with cyclists in mind, we would probably drive on the left as they do in Britain. Since you mount and dismount your bike on the left, in Britain you always have the bike between yourself and passing traffic. In cities and towns you can start with the bike in the street while you have a foot on the curb; in the States you would have to be on the street side of the bike.

To get maps in Britain, you must buy them; even the ordinary oil company maps are sold, not given away. Good maps are a necessity for cyclists. They want to find their way on narrow lanes and unpaved tracks; they want to know where the hills and valleys are, how steep a descent will be, and where the land is forested and where farmed. In England there are excellent maps which tell you all these things and much more.

The granddaddies of British maps are the government-produced Ordnance Survey (OS) maps. Their detail and printing are impeccable, but their usefulness for cycling is limited by their scale of approximately one and a quarter inch to the mile (1:50,000). Riding at even a moderate pace, you'd run through a map in a day. Occasionally though, if you're cycletouring from a fixed location or in an area like the Lake District, you'll appreciate the detail of the OS maps.

Bartholomew's half-inch-to-the-mile (1:126,720) maps are standard for cycletouring. The scale allows for good detail—even many footpaths are shown—

and the maps are color-keyed for elevation to allow easy use by those unaccustomed to standard contour maps. Despite the half-inch-to-the-mile scale, it takes only sixty-two maps to cover all of Great Britain. Bartholomew maps in the half-inch series can be ordered by CTC members from the club at a discount. Nonmembers can order from a map shop, or directly from the Bartholomew Company in Scotland. (See Appendix C for addresses.) It should be noted that the Bartholomew 1:126,720 (half-inch) maps are currently being converted to metric measurement; the comparable new maps will be on a scale of 1:100,000, but will still cover Britain in sixty-two sheets, so one can order from the old map index without confusion. The new metric maps cost 70p each.

Roads in Britain are identified by a letter followed by a number. The letter prefixes are *A*, *B* and *M*. *M* stands for motorway, what we would call a thruway or turnpike; pedal-cycles are banned from motorways. *A* roads were the major highways before the motorways were constructed. Most are still heavily traveled by trucks and cars and are best avoided by cyclists. *B* and unclassified roads are what the cyclist looks for; these crisscross the country, allowing one to get almost everywhere while enjoying quiet, traffic-free riding. Unclassified roads, those with no letter or number designation at all, are the least traveled of the paved roads. Most are in good repair.

One further refinement of the road numbering

SIGNPOSTING IS EXCELLENT IN ENGLAND——IT TAKES AN
EFFORT TO GET LOST. A ROADS ARE LIKE STATE HIGH-
WAYS IN THE U.S.; B ROADS ARE LIKE OUR SECONDARY
ROADS.

system should be mentioned; it applies to both A
and B roads. The more digits in the number following the letter, the less traffic the road is likely to have.
The A4 and A40 are major highways; the A3075 is
not. If a B is followed by four digits, the road should
have less traffic than a road designated by a B and
three digits.

The Bartholomew maps use a yellow color for most
B and unclassified roads. We strongly advise planning
routes that allow you to stay on these roads as much

as possible. Sometimes they follow a more direct course to your destination than major roads; but even when their way is devious, rarely will they add more than three or four miles in thirty to your ride. Meanwhile, you'll breathe clean air away from huge rumbling trucks, and you'll be further repaid for any extra mileage by much more pleasing scenery and visits to small bypassed villages.

Britain uses the standard international road signs, long in use on the Continent and just starting to ap-

MOST STEEP HILLS HAVE WARNING SIGNS SIMILAR TO THE ONE PICTURED. THE RATIO HERE INDICATES A VERY STEEP GRADE—ONE FOOT VERTICALLY FOR EVERY THREE FEET HORIZONTALLY.

pear on this side of the Atlantic. The signs use self-evident representational designs intended to cross language barriers. The only sign worth special mention is one which has a black triangle on a white background and a ratio like 1:6 or 1:7 on it. This warns of a steep hill—by the time you see the sign you'll know whether it's up or down. The numbers, 1:6 for example, indicate that the road drops, or climbs, one foot for every six it extends horizontally. Signs appear, usually, only for hills of 1:10 or steeper. With good, dry brakes, only hills from about 1:7 to 1:3 will cause much concern. With wet brakes, any hill can be dangerous. Even with dry brakes hills of 1:4 or 1:3 can cause more than a few anxious moments. It's often advisable to dismount for these. Use your judgment. If you have any reason to distrust your brakes, or your own stamina, get off and walk.

Though roads in England, even little-used ones, are well maintained and quite smooth, there are British cyclists who eschew even the most forgotten paved surfaces in favor of tracks and byways of stone, dirt, gravel or grass. These nominal riders shoulder their bikes over streams and mountain passes; some days they carry their bikes as much as the bikes carry them. The English call this kind of riding "rough stuff."

You need a strong back and a good pair of hiking boots for such goings-on. Though it does not suit everyone, the attraction of rough stuff is obvious. You let some air out of your tires, trade cycling shoes for

MANY BRITISH CYCLISTS "GET AWAY FROM IT ALL" ON MOUNTAIN TRACKS SUCH AS THIS ONE IN THE LAKE DISTRICT, NEAR GRASMERE.

walking shoes, and you can go almost anywhere. If you're carrying camping equipment, you might not see a car or another person for days. Most rough tracks are in mountainous areas, so quite naturally rough stuff is often combined with pass-storming—pushing yourself and your bike up rough but established mountain trails, crossing the high point at well-known passes, and plummeting (or walking) down the other side. The Lake District is a favorite area for pass-storming; the views are magnificent and most of the passes in Lakeland are unpaved.

Even conventional cyclists should ride a little mild rough stuff to see what it's like. You could start with a few unpaved miles of the Ridge Way in Berkshire and Wiltshire. More rugged cycle-campers can find wilderness enough in England to test their mettle; and after England, one can always move on to Scotland. If rough stuff sounds appealing, you might want to contact the Rough Stuff Fellowship. (See Appendix A for address.) Information about wilderness areas can also be obtained from the British Tourist Authority in this country, and from the Countryside Commission and the Ramblers' Association in England. (See Appendix B for addresses.)

There are times when even a bicycle seems to separate you too much from the land, and you want to set it aside for an hour, an afternoon or a whole day, and walk. Britain's thousands of miles of footpaths offer ample opportunity for pleasant rambles.

An American used to "Posted" and "No trespassing" signs everywhere is likely to be uncomfortable when a footpath leads across someone's back or front lawn or down their driveway to the road. But after you follow such a path a couple of times and get only a friendly wave from the landowner, you begin to relax.

One theory behind footpaths is quite simple: People walked paths into existence long before they thought they could "own" the land, so the right to use them predates and takes precedence over later claims. Most paths have been walked since the

IN ENGLAND "PRIVATE" DOES NOT ALWAYS MEAN WHAT IT DOES IN NORTH AMERICA. FOOTPATHS CROSS THOUSANDS OF SQUARE MILES OF PRIVATE LAND.

Middle Ages, and some were trod by Iron and Bronze Age walkers. Some paths record the shortest distance between village, pub, church and field; others, such as the Jurassic Way from the Humber in the northeast to the Mendips in the southwest or the Pilgrims Way from Dover to past Winchester, are long-distance paths first walked by prehistoric traders. There is no way of knowing exactly how old these and other long-distance paths are, but Bronze implements have been found along some. A few even predate the Bronze

Age. It is known that trading increased greatly in the Iron Age, and we can assume that a number of long-distance tracks date from that period.

Centuries of tradition were codified into law by the National Parks and Access to the Countryside Act of 1949. It is the public's right to use recognized footpaths, and it is illegal for a landowner, whether small farmer or lordly country gentleman, to obstruct a path. If there is an obstruction, a walker has the right, using a minimum of force, to remove it—though it might be wiser for a foreigner to merely report the matter to the parish or county authorities. The walker is on safe ground in crossing private property so long as he keeps to the footpath, makes no fires and commits no willful damage. In fact, a footpath has the legal status of a public highway.

In all, there are over 103,000 miles of footpaths and bridleways in England and Wales, or two miles of paths for every square mile. Footpaths are restricted to walkers (bicycles may be walked but not ridden), while bridleways are open to walkers, horsemen and cyclists. Though some footpaths have their origins lost in the past, the government is still buying land and acquiring rights-of-way for new ones. Most effort is being devoted to long-distance paths across vast, largely unspoiled sections of Britain. The Pennine Way is two hundred and fifty miles long, running from Edale in Derbyshire north along the Pennines to Hadrian's Wall and the Cheviot Hills in Scotland. In Devon and Cornwall, the Southwest Peninsula Coast Path is over five hundred miles long.

This cliff-edge path is especially grand, and not a little frightening, on the section along the north coast. Cyclists should give their saddles a rest occasionally and walk some of Britain's footpaths. Information on bridleways and footpaths can be obtained from the Countryside Commission. (See Appendix B for address.)

5/Where to Tour

In discussing possible touring areas, it seems best to take our bearings from London, since the capital is the starting place for most overseas visitors.

The Southeast. South and east of London, divided between the counties of Kent, Surrey and Sussex, are the rolling hills of the North and South Downs and the Weald. Cycling here is not strenuous, though the low hills offer pleasing variety. Because most of the region lies between London and the busy Channel coast, major roads carry heavy traffic and should be avoided. Similarly, much of the Channel coast itself is strung with popular resorts and is best approached warily, especially in the summer months. Inland from the heavily populated coast, one finds surprising quiet amid heath and forest.

Kent has been called the garden of England. The clay soil of the Weald supports thousand of acres of orchards growing apples, pears, cherries, strawberries, and in the Medway Valley, hops. The hops grow on vines supported to a height of twenty-five feet by posts; they are dried in nearby conical oasthouses. Proximity to London has made Kent popular with great families over the centuries, creating a legacy of stately homes. Among them are Knole; Penshurst Place, birthplace of Sir Philip Sidney; Ightham Mote; and on a smaller scale, Winston Churchill's country home, Chartwell, near Tunbridge Wells. Other famous figures associated with the southeast are Defoe, Dickens, Kipling, G. K. Chesterton and Hilaire Belloc.

The southeast enjoys a good—from the cyclist's point of view—rainfall record. The average is between twenty-five and thirty inches a year. March, April and May are the driest months; October through December the wettest. High temperatures in August average about 75°F., lows in January about 35°F.

Wessex. The old Saxon kingdom of Wessex included the region southwest of London embracing Hampshire, Wiltshire, Dorset and small parts of neighboring counties. This area has long been inhabited by people and contains some of history's most astounding works. Stonehenge and Avebury are perhaps the best known of the many relics of prehistoric people to be discovered in the region of Salisbury Plain, Wiltshire. The Middle Ages contributed the cathedrals at Winchester and Salisbury as well as a scattering of now ruined abbeys. The

Renaissance added two of England's greatest houses —Wilton House, where Shakespeare was a frequent visitor, and Longleat, whose library contains a copy of the First Folio of his plays. The chalk hills, or downs, which comprise much of Wessex, are a delight to cycle through. They are rounded, clothed and softened by rich grass, and sculptured to form dry valleys. Bleating sheep and singing skylarks animate a scene which is rural without seeming lonely, hilly but not exhausting. Atop the downs the air is usually light, cool and bracing—perfect for cycling. Even apart from sites of special interest to be seen along the way, it would be hard to think of a more suitable region for cycling than the downs of Wessex.

Hampshire's New Forest also offers relatively easy but varied cycling. The Forest has been largely without fences ever since it was a hunting reserve of William the Conqueror, and cyclists and motorists still share the roads with ponies, cows and other livestock. Though only about eighty miles from London, parts of the Forest seem like a wilderness hundreds of miles from civilization.

Rainfall is generally under thirty inches a year in Wessex. May tends to be the driest month and, with June and July, shares the record for the highest average number of hours of sunlight daily, just under eight.

Cotswolds. North of Wessex, the Cotswold Hills cover an area not more than thirty by forty miles, roughly from Oxford west to Cheltenham and from

IN THE NEW FOREST, HAMPSHIRE, LIVESTOCK ARE FREE TO GO PRETTY MUCH WHERE THEY PLEASE. THE FOREST HAS BEEN WITHOUT FENCES SINCE THE TIME OF WILLIAM THE CONQUEROR.

Cirencester north to Broadway. Oxford is about sixty miles northwest of London, about an hour's journey by British Rail.

Though the much acclaimed beauty of the Cotswold hills and villages attracts many visitors from Britain and abroad, there are few signs that the region is any the worse for wear. Commercial exploitation is virtually nonexistent. Villages dot the landscape, and each keeps compactly to its historic ground; there is no spillover along roads or into the countryside.

Many villages are built entirely of the famed gold-honey-colored Cotswold limestone, which shines gloriously in the sun and is a bit cheery even in rain. In the late Middle Ages, the wool trade made the region rich, and sheep are still plentiful on its hills.

The Cotswolds abound in small paved lanes used by few motor vehicles and excellent for cycling. Though none of the hills is over eight hundred feet, there are few stretches of level ground, and the constant up and down makes for riding somewhat more

BIBURY, GLOUCESTERSHIRE, IS ONE OF THE MOST VISITED AND PHOTOGRAPHED VILLAGES IN THE COTSWOLDS. THE WATER IS THE RIVER COLN, A CLEAR, COLD TROUT STREAM.

vigorous than the modest height of the hills might suggest. As the area is small and villages are close together, cyclists can find plenty to see while riding very modest distances each day.

What's there to see in the Cotswolds? First and most importantly, the beauty of the region itself— hills, villages, parish churches, farms, streams and sky. Some of the more acclaimed villages are Fairford, Bibury, Bourton-on-the-Water, Stow-on-the-Wold, Lower Slaughter and Broadway. But scores of others await discovery. Other attractions include Blenheim Palace, near Woodstock, and the castles at Warwick and Kenilworth, about a day's ride to the north. Stratford-upon-Avon is best visited in seasons other than summer, when it is mobbed by tourists.

East Anglia. Completing our circle of cycling areas within a short distance of London, to the north and east we come to East Anglia, including parts of Essex and Cambridgeshire as well as Norfolk and Suffolk, originally the North Folk and South Folk of the ancient kingdom of East Anglia. Although this region does not attract a lot of tourists, it should not be dismissed quickly by the cyclist.

East Anglia is largely flat. "Boring," says the motorist; "easy pedaling," a cyclist might reply. The general flatness plus an overall dearth of cars in this sparsely populated area add up to relaxing, enjoyable riding, especially for inexperienced or older cyclists. Quiet lanes connect villages, many of whose houses are washed the traditional pink and many of whose inhabitants still worship in fine parish churches endowed by Flemish weavers who settled here in the Middle Ages. Dutch influence is seen in many older houses and in bulb fields stretching to the horizon.

English, German and Dutch vacationers frequent a few busy East Anglian coastal resorts. The other major attraction of the region is the university town of Cambridge. The sea-bathing resorts might be best avoided by cyclists, but Cambridge is a delight. Beyond Cambridge you can go your own way enjoying the sight and sound of a vast variety of bird life and great, expansive views of sky and cloud such as those which inspired the painter John Constable. Statistically at least, one is likely to ride under sunny skies, as this is the driest region in England. There were once hundreds of windmills in East Anglia; a few remain, and a working mill can be seen at Saxtead Green, near Framlingham. If you infer from this that you may encounter strong breezes here, you will be correct. But the breeze brings air clean and fresh.

The Southwest.   Farther afield from London, but not more than three hours away by British Rail, are the southwestern counties of Somerset, Devon and Cornwall. The southwest draws more vacationers from other parts of the British Isles than any holiday area in England. Nonetheless, the southwest should not be missed for fear of congestion and traffic; even on holiday weekends most narrow, out-of-the-way roads are ignored as the vast majority of visitors follow highways to the well-known resorts such as Torquay and Newquay.

Cycling in the southwest is varied and at times exciting. Experienced cyclists will enjoy the challenges of the cliff-bordered north coast of Devon and Cornwall. Equally energetic riding can be experienced in the Mendip and Quantock Hills and on Dartmoor, Exmoor and Bodmin Moor. Less vigorous riders can also sample the beauties of the southwest. The Somerset Levels, between the Mendips and Quantocks, are almost totally flat; the south coast of Devon and Cornwall is more gentle than the north; and the moors can be skirted as well as assaulted directly. Or, one can slowly climb Dartmoor, for example, and find enough of interest atop it to repay spending a few days there.

Of the southwest's three moors, Dartmoor is the largest and the most conducive to cycling. The moor is particularly rich in relics of prehistoric people, though similarly interesting archeological sites are found in various parts of Devon and Cornwall. Somerset is a bit more "civilized" than its western neighbors and boasts fine cathedrals at Wells and Bath and magnificent ruins at Glastonbury. Traffic in Bath is undeniably bad, but the city offers so much—from Roman baths to eighteenth-century terraces and crescents—that it shouldn't be bypassed.

The southwest gets lots of rain, the uplands being particularly wet. May and June are usually the driest months; June averages eight hours of sun daily. Because of the influence of the sea, winters in Devon and Cornwall are the mildest in Britain. January high temperatures average just over 50°F.

Yorkshire. In the north of England, Yorkshire is

THE BLEAKNESS OF DARTMOOR IS BROKEN BY ONE FIELD
AND A HOUSE AND BARN. THE GRANITE OUTCROP IN THE
FOREGROUND IS PART OF HOOKNEY TOR.

much visited by cyclists. The county is England's
largest and contains everything from a long coastline
to a chain of mountains with peaks well over two
thousand feet. It also has York, a big city with
medieval charm, as well as scores of interesting towns
and villages.

For cyclists, interest in Yorkshire centers on the
Dales. These are valleys cut in the Pennine chain by
the action of flowing water. As you ride beside a
stream, great rounded green, brown and purple

mountains rise on either side of you; as you climb, you enjoy views, as from a glider or hot-air balloon, of a patchwork of stone walls, green fields and brown wastelands, dotted with white sheep and gray slate roofs. Riding in the Dales is characterized by long, gradual ascents and descents. The Dales are not the place for an out-of-shape rider, but the gradual rise of most roads allows them to be climbed by pedaling rather than walking.

Of the Yorkshire Dales, Wharfedale is probably the

RUINED ABBEYS ARE NOT UNCOMMON IN RURAL ENGLAND. THIS IS BYLAND ABBEY IN YORKSHIRE, A COUNTY PARTICULARLY RICH IN MONASTIC RUINS.

most visited, while to the north Swaledale is one of the most rugged. Wensleydale, Airedale, Dentdale and the others each has its own character and devotees. Rain is spread evenly through the year in Yorkshire; riders in the Dales should be aware of the possibility of heavy snow from December through March.

To the east of the Vale of York is the other great upland of the region, the North York Moors. The Moors are perhaps less spectacular than the Dales, but they too offer good cycling—of a slightly less strenuous sort. Here Farndale is most known, both for the pretty village of Hutton-le-Hole and for the profusion of daffodils which seem to pave miles of the dale in April. At the far end of the warm season, September is the best month for seeing the high moors clothed in purple heather.

In addition to its natural beauty, Yorkshire claims the finest concentration of abbey ruins in England. Chief among these are Rievaulx, Jervaulx, Fountains, Whitby and Bolton.

Lake District. West of the Yorkshire Dales rise the most written-about, visited and the highest mountains in England—those of the Lake District. Even less than the Dales is this the place for a novice to begin cycling; but Lakeland is without doubt to be enjoyed by any reasonably fit cyclist who has had a recent heart checkup. The whole of Lakeland is only about thirty miles in diameter; yet this area holds more than twenty-five youth hostels and numerous hotels and bed-and-breakfast places.

Perhaps the key to enjoying Lakeland is to set your sights small. Plan to ride ten miles in a day, or five. Walk a lot. If you find a pleasant place, stay for a couple of days and explore the vicinity on foot. Follow the British; they've spent two centuries cultivating the proper way to savor the Lake District on foot.

Windermere and Derwent Water are the most popular lakes, and the Ambleside-Grasmere-Keswick road is usually too crowded for comfortable cycling. If there seem to be too many people about, try moving west or east of this central region. If possible, it is, of course, best to visit Lakeland before July or after August.

In all months the region is subject to heavy rains, which turn to heavy snow in the cold months. Storms gather notoriously quickly in the Lake District, and it is possible to become stranded, especially if cycling off paved roads. Carrying emergency food is a reasonable precaution. And it is also reasonable to be very wary of trusting wet brakes on mountain roads.

Needless to add, the list of touring areas suggested does not exhaust the regions of England suited to cycletouring. You might plan a tour to take in one or more regions, or you might ignore a regional basis for planning altogether and plan a tour around a geographical feature or a special interest. There are many routes of this kind which lend themselves to cycletouring. You might want to follow a river, such as the Severn, Wye or Cam, or one of the old canals, perhaps the Kennet and Avon or the Shropshire Union. Tracing the route of ancient roads can also make for an interesting tour. Some prehistoric long-distance routes which can still be followed in part or whole are the Jurassic Way, the Pilgrims Way, the Ridge Way and the Icknield Way. Traceable Roman roads include the Fosse Way, Stane Street and Watling Street. Perusing literature on England will undoubtedly suggest other possibilities.

Wherever you decide to tour, you'll probably be getting there by British Rail. Below are some favored cycletouring areas along with suggested starting points. Fares given are for adults one-way, second class from London. Add one half the adult fare for your bicycle. Riding times and fares are approximate and subject to change.

TOURING AREA	STARTING POINT	FARE ($)	TIME (hrs.)
Southeast, Wessex	Winchester or	6	1¼
	Gatwick Airport	3	40 min.
	or Canterbury	5	1½
Southwest	Exeter	13	3
	Bath	9	2
Cotswolds	Oxford	6	1¼
Vale of Severn, South Wales	Cheltenham	10	2½
East Anglia	Cambridge	5	1¼
Shropshire, North Wales	Shrewsbury	14	3
Yorkshire	York	17	3

Lake District	Kendal or	22	4½
	Carlisle	25	5¼
Scottish Border, Lowlands	Carlisle	25	5¼

In suggesting possible cycletouring areas, at least brief mention should be made of the so-called Celtic fringe—Ireland, Wales and Scotland.

The quickest and least expensive ferries to Ireland leave from Holyhead and Fishguard in Wales. The crossing from Liverpool to Dublin takes six hours. Ireland is a poor country with fewer paved small roads than England. But this doesn't affect the cyclist very much, since there is little traffic even on main roads in Ireland, except for tourist traffic at the height of the season.

Unless there is something of special interest to you in the east of the country, we'd suggest taking the train to Cork or Galway and working your way up or down the rugged, wild, primitive and wet west coast. Much of the west of Ireland is as wild as the Aran Islands, a rocky land where poverty wears a green, flowered mantle. See Robert Flaherty's film *Man of Aran* and read J. M. Synge's *Aran Islands* or Maurice O'Sullivan's *Twenty Years A-Growing*; then get to counties Clare, Galway and Kerry before the donkey carts disappear and the old men start wearing gloves in winter instead of worn wool socks.

In addition to being poor, Wales is mountainous. Thus few paved roads cross it. The north and south coasts are crowded and industrial with busy high-

THIS IS NEAR THE TIP OF THE DINGLE PENINSULA, CO.
KERRY, IRELAND. BEYOND THE WATER ARE THE IVERAGH
MOUNTAINS, PART OF THE FAMED RING OF KERRY.

ways offering scant cycling pleasure. But if you love
mountains, just stay away from the coasts and that's
about all you'll see. Mount Snowdon, in Snowdonia
National Park, is the highest point in all of England
and Wales.

Wales is a strange, suspicious, superstitious place
with the oddest, longest names you'll find anywhere.
And the people themselves are not a little strange.

Scotland is like Ireland in that you don't have to
talk people into going there. Those who love the

place know they do, and there's no convincing those who don't.

Cyclists thinking about touring in Scotland should be prepared for rain, drizzle and cool temperatures, even in summer. They should also be prepared for energetic to strenuous cycling. The Scottish Lowlands are "low" only in comparison with the Highlands. The bed-and-breakfast cyclist can get around the Lowlands fairly well, but large areas of the Highlands, especially the Northwest Highlands of counties Sutherland and Ross and Cromarty, should be attempted only by cycle-campers. This area is one of the last remaining great wildernesses in Europe. The country is beautiful, but challenging and potentially dangerous for the inexperienced.

If you take one of the larger ferries to Ireland or the Continent, try to take the kind that has drive-on service for vehicles. You can ride your bike aboard a drive-on ferry, lock it in an out-of-the-way spot, unload your bags, and go to your seat or cabin. (If you aren't counting pennies too closely, you'll be much happier if you take a cabin for overnight voyages.) Ferries without drive-on facilities lift cars aboard with cranes and, believe it or not, your thirty-pound bike will be loaded in the same way. Needless to say, spokes and other parts do not take well to such treatment. We first encountered a crane-loading ferry on a return trip from Ireland. When we saw what they wanted to do with our bikes, we charged frantically up the chain of command of the ship until we got to a sympathetic former cyclist. He let us push the bikes aboard ourselves, but probably only because it was off-season and the ship was almost empty. In any season, take a crane-loading ferry only if there's absolutely no other choice.

Hovercraft should not be counted on. They have limited space and take cycles only in the off-season with advance booking. There are some concessions for CTC members; check with CTC Travel in London. (See Appendix B for address.)

As you ride within England, you're likely to have opportunities to take smaller ferries. Along the coast they often cross estuaries, bays and rivers. Some of these crossings are as short as a hundred yards and cost only a few pence; others can range up to a couple of miles. Most provide worthwhile shortcuts, allowing cyclists to rest while avoiding miles of extra riding around obstructing waterways. If you want to cycle around the Scottish islands, you'll have to make many ferry crossings. The CTC *Handbook* has a list of all the ferries serving the British Isles with information on fares and schedules.

6/Finding Food and Lodging

England offers an abundance of inexpensive accommodations. One of the pleasures of touring there is meeting people quite easily and naturally by staying in their homes. To do this you don't have to apply to any special "meet the people" program— all you have to do is stay in some of the thousands of bed-and-breakfast (b-and-b) places you'll find almost everywhere.

"Bed-and-breakfast" means exactly what the name implies; for a set price (averaging about £2, or $4.60, per person, outside London) you get a place to sleep and breakfast, usually a large, filling one. This is one of the best bargains in England. It's even better for cyclists, since in rural areas you usually pay the least and get the best breakfasts.

Most bed-and-breakfast places are private homes —attached town houses, suburban single-family units or farm houses. Many widows, left with extra bedrooms and small incomes, do b-and-b. Similarly, many young families and farmers can use some extra cash. But you'll also find people doing b-and-b who don't seem to need the money. Well-to-do people may do it because they're lonely, or just for the sake of meeting new people. A few do it as a public service of sorts, providing inexpensive lodging for travelers.

B-and-b can be found throughout Britain, from London to the smallest hamlet. Except for certain resort areas, prices go down substantially once you leave the bigger cities. In regions with a fair amount of tourism, such as the southwest and the Lake District, even isolated farmers do b-and-b. It's harder to find such places in the wealthy counties surrounding London.

There is no complete list of all the people doing b-and-b in Britain. Even if there were, it would be too bulky for a cyclist to carry. A good, brief guide to b-and-b is included in the CTC *Handbook*. With over three thousand listings, it is a useful, but by no means complete, guide. If the *Handbook* lists two or three places to stay in a town, you can usually assume there will be others and that you won't have trouble finding a vacancy somewhere. If there are none listed for a place, it doesn't mean that none exist, but you should be wary of arriving there just before nightfall.

When you arrive at a town or village where you want to stay, you can start looking for signs saying "Bed and Breakfast" or "B & B," but only about half

BLEASE HALL, WESTMORLAND, A TUDOR STRUCTURE NOW
USED AS A FARMHOUSE AND BED-AND-BREAKFAST ESTAB-
LISHMENT. THE ABSENCE OF WINDOWS RESULTS FROM
THE ATTEMPTS OF EARLIER OWNERS TO AVOID THE
WINDOW TAX.

the places doing b-and-b have signs out. To find the
others, you have to know about them in advance, or
ask. You should always ask; try people on the street,
storekeepers, policemen. If you inquire at a place
that's full, ask if they can recommend some other
b-and-b in the neighborhood. Many of the best places
have no signs out, so it's worth doing a little local
survey to find out what's available.

their share. Most hostels are beautifully situated and well run. A few are in historic buildings—one occupies a Norman castle—while others use specially built modern facilities. Overnight 1975 rates for senior hostelers (age twenty-one and over) range from 54p ($1.25) in the Simple grade hostel to £1.00 ($2.30) in the Special grade. In between are Standard grade for 65p and Superior at 80p. Rates for junior hostelers (age sixteen to twenty-one) range from 46p to 80p. These rates are for hostels outside London and do not include breakfast. For further information write to either AYH or YHA. (See Appendix A for addresses.)

If you are cycle-camping, you can pitch your tent on the grounds of some youth hostels for one-half the regular overnight charge. There are campgrounds in most popular tourist areas, and there is even a special section set aside exclusively for lightweight campers (backpackers and cycle-campers) in the New Forest National Park in Hampshire. In rural areas you can simply ask a farmer for permission to put your tent in a corner of his field. You'll rarely be rejected, except in very popular regions like the Lake District, where tents would soon crowd out livestock if farmers assented to such requests.

Even if you hostel or camp most of the time, it's worth the extra money to stay in bed-and-breakfast places at least a few times. You'll get a look at ordinary life in a foreign country which you may remember longer and which may mean more to you than your visit to Westminster Abbey or Stonehenge.

It is easier to find a place to sleep in England than it is to find a well-prepared, reasonably nutritious meal. Someone once remarked that the English seem to regard food for themselves in the same way they do petrol for their automobiles: Both are necessities, but it is absurd to expect either to be particularly tasty. Outside of the cities, it is sometimes hard to get a meal of any kind in the evening. Snacks you will find in abundance, everything from pickled onions to baked beans on toast, but it takes some thought and foresight to obtain a reasonably balanced diet and to avoid going to bed hungry occasionally.

Nonetheless, most days in England start well in terms of food; a "full English breakfast" will be included in the price of the room almost everywhere you stay. As with most things that have to do with food, the quality improves as you get into the countryside. If you stay at a farm, you are likely to get fresh milk, free-range eggs and freshly baked bread. You will often be provided with an abundance of food, which, if you are not accustomed to large breakfasts, may seem impossible to handle. But such a meal gets you off to an energetic start; and, because of its high fat and protein content, can keep you going all through the morning and sometimes longer.

You will usually get a choice of juice or cereal (in the country you will often receive both, sometimes with fresh fruit replacing the juice); then one or two eggs; sausage or bacon or both; stewed tomatoes; and a good supply of toast and tea—both of which are often replenished until you put a stop to it. Tea (or coffee, if you choose) does little for you nutritionally, but it does warm you on cold mornings in unheated breakfast rooms. The British are not big milk drinkers and will rarely offer a glass of milk unless you ask for it. Short of that, choosing cereal always brings a generous pitcher of milk, and you can always drink the milk provided for use in tea.

If you choose to hostel or camp, you will, of course, have to provide your own breakfast. But these filling English breakfasts are a good reason to take advantage of the b-and-b custom, at least occasionally.

For lunch it is best to supply yourself at grocery stores, either at night or early in the morning. Most towns have supermarkets, and small villages and hamlets at least have a post-office store which carries the basics. British cheeses are quite good: Double Gloucester, Cheddar, Wensleydale, Leicester, Caerphilly and Cheshire are all mild cheeses, good for sandwiches and for eating alone. Healthy loaves of unsliced whole wheat bread can be found in most food stores, though the widest selection of the best bread can be had in a bakery. You will always be able to get apples and oranges; pears, grapes and grapefruit are available most of the time, plus other fruits in season. Cakes and cookies (biscuits, in England) are British specialties; even packaged ones are surprisingly good, while fresh from a bakery they are mouth-watering delights. Whenever possible, it's best to buy from specialty shops rather than super-

IN SMALL VILLAGES THE POST OFFICE SERVES VARIOUS
FUNCTIONS. MOST COMMONLY IT IS THE LOCAL GROCERY
STORE; IN LODERS, DORSET, IT ALSO HOUSES THE BUTCHER
SHOP.

markets. Bread and cakes are best from bakeries,
fruit from the greengrocer, and so on. Nonetheless,
if you stick to these types of luncheon foods you will
find good quality even in large supermarkets and
small post-office stores.

The problem of finding an evening meal is mini-
mized in areas like the southwest (Devon and Cornwall) and the Lake District, where most bed-and-

breakfast places offer an optional evening meal. (If you want this full meal, ask for a dinner or evening meal; "supper" in England refers to a snack taken shortly before bedtime.) We strongly advise taking advantage of this home-cooked meal whenever it is offered. Like breakfast, it is usually prepared well, with many courses and generous portions. You may hesitate because you won't know ahead of time what will be served, but the English repertory is not too extensive: If it isn't beef or lamb, it will probably be chicken; occasionally, you'll be served ham or fish. The dessert (sweet) is often the highpoint of the meal; many English people seem to regard the main course as mere prelude.

The atmosphere at evening meal is usually homey and relaxed, and you'll have a leisurely opportunity to chat with other guests. The added price for the evening meal will average £1.25 ($2.90) and is well worth it in terms of quality, quantity and, above all, convenience. If you want to take advantage of the evening-meal option you should plan to stop riding by mid-afternoon, so the people with whom you are staying will have time to prepare. Occasionally, we've not stopped riding until six o'clock and were eating a meal at seven, but getting a meal on such short notice cannot be counted on.

If the evening-meal option prevailed throughout England, eating would be reasonably easy. Unfortunately, it is only rural areas with a heavy tourist business which maintain this happy custom. Elsewhere, getting a meal at the end of the day is usually a problem. In many smaller towns, restaurants close at around six o'clock, just when you begin looking for a meal—and most of the grocery stores close then, too.

What can you do? Luckily, many (though not all) pubs serve food, and every village, no matter how small, has its pub. Some pubs put a menu out next to the door, others have a sign saying they serve food. These are hopeful signs but never sure indications that you'll really be able to get something to eat. Once inside you may find that the menu or sign refers only to lunch, that "no one's in the kitchen today," or that it's an old sign to which no one pays the slightest attention. Some pub owners may take pity on you and scrape up something, others will not.

Perhaps about half the time you will be able to get some kind of food at a pub. This will range from soup and sandwiches and "basket snacks" (most often fried chicken or fish and chips) to a full and sometimes well-prepared meal. When you find a pub which does serve a full meal, it will probably be the best English food you will eat outside of a private home.

Most pub food however, particularly the bar snack type, lacks variety and is devoid of vegetables. Though it may be enjoyable to have a sandwich, peanuts and beer for an occasional dinner, you cannot depend on such meals to keep you alive and pedaling on an extended trip. For more variety and often better-prepared, healthier food, we'd recommend choosing a foreign restaurant over most English restaurants or pubs. Probably the most widely available foreign food in England is Chinese. You'll find Chinese restaurants not only in large cities and towns, but even in obscure places you were certain hadn't been seen by a foreigner until you arrived. Here you can enjoy a healthy meal with crisp vegetables, fried rice, and meat, chicken or fish.

Although a light lunch and a cooked evening meal usually fit best into a cyclist's day, there are times when it is advisable to have your big meal at noon. If you are staying in a town for a day or two, not cycling, you will find better bargains and more choice if you eat your lunch out in a restaurant. Many towns that abound in little tearoom-type restaurants will leave you, after six o'clock, with no place to eat but the local pub. These small establishments catering to lunch and tea-time guests often serve reasonably good food at moderate prices, though they're likely to put most effort into their desserts. If you order tea, remember that it will automatically be served with milk in it. If you don't want milk, be sure to ask for black tea.

Those times when you're getting a "bargain" lunch might be good opportunities to indulge in local or seasonal specialties. Strawberries with fresh cream is a classic English delicacy that shouldn't be missed; it can be had in late spring and early summer. Pies and crumbles made with newly picked berries can be eaten in rural places throughout the warmer months. In the southwest desserts will be covered with clotted cream, a very thick sweet cream about the consistency of our sour cream. Somerset is known for apple cider. If you're in England at Christmas, you should try the traditional plum pudding. Yorkshire pudding is well known, but rarely prepared well these days.

Despite your best efforts, there may be times when you cannot get an evening meal for days running. We twice had this experience in the Yorkshire Dales. In such a situation it's best to try to get a cooked meal at noon; or else resign yourself to eating two picnic-style meals a day. Even without cooking facilities, you can do pretty well at getting some variety and nutritional balance in your picnic meals. Canned (tinned) fish, such as Norwegian brisling, a sardine, are excellent sources of protein and can be balanced by fresh bread, yogurt and canned or fresh fruit. Some supermarkets have counters where you can get prepared salads and coleslaw; these range from good to not so good. If a quick look around a town tells you that only the fish and chips stand will be open after six o'clock, you'd be wise to get to the grocery store before it closes and buy your supper there.

One good thing about British restaurants is that they all have their menus beside the door or in the window. So even if there's only a limited choice of indifferently prepared food, at least you'll know what it will cost.

To sum up: Breakfasts are no problem. Lunches can be quite good if you buy good ingredients at the dairy, bakery and greengrocer. Dinners can present problems. Take an evening meal in a private home whenever it is offered; choose a foreign (Chinese, Indian, Greek, Italian or whatever) restaurant when you can; beware of restaurant closing times; most pubs serve food, some don't; and, prepare to be self-sufficient some nights.

7/On-the-Road Repairs

Basically, a bicycle is a simple machine. There's nothing much that can go wrong with it, and most of the things that do go wrong require only common sense to fix. Almost all the moving parts on a derailleur-equipped cycle are clearly visible and easy to get at. If a problem arises and you lack the appropriate tool or spare part, don't panic. If there's a house nearby, give it a try. The owner might have what you need or know where you can get it. At the least he'll probably let you leave your bike safely in his garage or shed while you hitch or take a bus to the nearest town that has a cycle shop.

Aside from the possibility of a bad smashup, most of the things that go wrong with a ten-speed bike have to do simply with parts wearing out—and thus can be anticipated. Any cable, brake or derailleur might break, as could a spoke. Carry spares. An extra toe strap weighs little and will save discomfort should one break. Nuts may eventually work loose, particularly on newly fitted luggage carriers. A couple of spare nuts take up almost no space and can save headaches if you lose one. What else can wear out? Not much. A bad fall can end the life of a rear derailleur, but with a chain rivet extractor handy, you can shorten the chain to fit tightly over chainring and freewheel cogs without a derailleur. Pedaling along using one speed is better than being stranded. The power chain itself will rarely snap in normal use, and if it does, it's easily fixed provided you have a rivet extractor along.

Basic maintenance. 1. If your seatpost has an open top, as many do, cover it with plastic electrical tape before leaving home, and replace the tape if it comes loose. This will keep water, grit and everything else from getting down the seat tube. Some bikes, but not all, have a liner inside the seat tube to prevent foreign objects from falling into the bottom bracket. These objects can quickly ruin a very expensive bottom bracket assembly once they have found their way into it.

2. Each day before you start to ride, give your bike a quick inspection. Check pressure in tires. Loose nuts should be discovered before they can do any damage. You may even spot a frayed cable, but these usually break insidiously at places you can't see, so never be overconfident.

3. It's difficult to keep a bike polished and dirt-

free while on the road day after day, but the cleaner it is, the less wear it will suffer. Polishing may be optional, but carrying an oil can is not. Take along a can of oil and use it regularly. The chain should have a drop of oil placed on each roller after every heavy rain or soaking it endures. Excess oil may hold excess dirt and make the chain an unsightly mess, but that's better than letting it rust. A drop of oil on the moving parts of the front and rear derailleurs will keep them in good working order. Remember the pivots of the rear one as well as the rollers. The latter should normally be packed with grease; but on the road, where grease is unavailable, oil is better than nothing. In spells of bad weather, you'll be oiling frequently, as rain washes both grease and oil from moving parts.

Tire care. A simple but important step in preventing problems from developing is to keep tires properly inflated. This is especially important with the extra weight a tourist carries. Less expensive air pumps with a rubber and cloth connector between pump and tube valve must be used vigorously. Pressure must be built up by rapid, hard pumping. If you do this and check that the connector is tight, they perform adequately. Better pumps, such as the Silca, are designed with a head that fits directly over the tube's valve stem. An airtight fit is insured by a rubber gasket inside the head. Since this kind of pump and the Presta valve are not very familiar to users of clincher tires in the States—but are common in England—we'll explain briefly how they work.

1. Move wheel until valve is pointed straight down from the twelve o'clock position.

2. Remove the dust cap and open the screw of the Presta valve. Push the screw in for a second, letting a little air escape, to make sure the valve is free.

3. Here's the tricky part: Quickly shove the pump head over the valve. A frightening amount of air may seem to escape. Keep pushing until the noise of escaping air stops. Then hold the pump in place on the valve with one hand, and pump with the other. This is awkward at first and takes some practice.

4. When you have enough air in the tire, the pump must be *knocked* from its secure position on the valve. Hold the pump with one hand and give it a solid blow with the side of the fist as close to the valve as you can get. Don't try to work the pump off gently—you'll only let air escape and have to start again, and you could break the valve stem completely.

Fixing a flat. Surely the most common on-the-road repair is fixing a flat tire. With clincher tires you're really fixing a punctured tube. The following instructions are for clincher (wired-on) tires, the kind most tourists use.

1. Remove the wheel from the bike.

2. Pry the bead (wire) of the tire over the rim edge with a tire iron ("tire lever" in Britain). Then carefully work the other iron under the bead beside the first one. Slowly move the irons in opposite directions, forcing more of the bead over the rim. As you go, be

careful not to pinch or rip the tube with the irons. A tiny puncture is repairable, but a long rip is not.

3. When the tire is off one side of the rim, push the valve of the tube through the hole in the rim and remove the tube. If you have a spare along, use it and repair the damaged tube at your leisure. If not, you'll have to patch the tube on the road. Simply follow the directions that come with your tire patch kit: Locate the hole, clean the area around it, apply one or two coats of rubber cement, let dry and rub on the patch.

4. While you have access to the inside of the rim, inspect it for protruding spokes and remove all the rust you can. If possible, dust the new tube and tire interior with talcum powder. This will absorb moisture and allow the tube to slip unrestrictedly into its natural position within the tire.

5. Introduce the new tube valve through the rim hole and fit it onto the rim. Then, *by hand*, start forcing the tire bead back over the rim. As you go make sure that the tube valve is still straight—pointing directly at the hub center. The last couple of inches may be difficult to force on, but persevere. If you do it without tire irons you can be sure of not damaging your new tube.

6. Once the tire is back on the rim, inflate slowly. Check to be sure the tire is seated evenly and firmly on the rim all the way around. You may have to work with it around the valve. Most tires have a design on their wall to let you judge how much of it is under the edge of the rim.

Broken spokes. If only one spoke breaks, you can almost certainly keep riding for the rest of the day at least. However, most times the wheel will be knocked out of true, so make sure it doesn't rub constantly on a brake block. If it does, try adjusting the brakes so there is a wider space between the blocks for the rim to pass through. When the time comes to replace the spoke, you won't have much of a job unless the broken spoke attaches to the hub on the freewheel side of the rear wheel. Unfortunately, because the spokes on the freewheel side of derailleur-equipped bikes are under the greatest tension, they are the ones most likely to break. If this is where your damaged spoke is, you'll have to remove the freewheel (with your indispensable freewheel remover) before proceeding to the following steps.

1. Remove wheel from bike and remove tire, tube and rim tape from the wheel.

2. Before removing it, note carefully the way the broken spoke is woven through the other spokes. Then take the broken spoke out and introduce the replacement spoke, starting it through the drilled hole in the hub. Thread the replacement spoke through the other spokes so that its position is identical to that of the spoke it is replacing.

3. Screw the spoke into the nipple, which you have pushed through the hole in the rim. The nipple tightens left-handed, opposite to the way you might at first expect.

4. Tighten the new spoke until its tension approximates that of the other spokes. Twanging the

spokes like guitar strings is the best simple way to judge tension.

5. Before replacing the rim tape and tube, make sure that the end of the new spoke is not protruding from the nipple. If it is, you'll have an instant flat. A protruding spoke *must* be filed down. You could sacrifice a nail file to the task. We've made do with rocks and the perforated edges of heavy British coins—the 10p piece is ideal.

Replacing broken cables. If you have to replace any cable you should remember two things: First, look carefully at the route followed by the broken cable before removing it, and second, never snip off the end of any cable to shorten it until it is fitted and in place—and then snip only if you must. Once a cable is snipped, the end frays and it's almost impossible to get it through eyeholes and cable housings again.

Brake cables must be started at the brake lever end. There's usually nothing complicated about them, but sometimes they have to be worked through quite a length of cable housing. Bathing the cable with grease or oil before starting makes it slide more easily. When you're finished, the brakes will have to be adjusted anew. Then pull good and hard on the brake levels and make sure nothing slips.

Derailleur cables generally have less housing to go through, and in that way are easier to work with than brake cables. While you remove the screw securing the gear-shift lever, keep a hand holding it in position. Then slowly and carefully take it apart. You'll often be surprised at how many thin washers are inside the simple-looking lever. Watch where each piece comes from and put it back there. The only other thing to mention is that the nut holding the shift cable to the rear derailleur must be quite tight. It's surprising how much tension this cable is under— it will slip unless the nut is very secure.

You shouldn't assume that most of the repairs described in this chapter are likely to be required while on tour. Most times, fixing a flat tire is the only repair that comes up, and you can cycle thousands of miles without even having to do that.

Appendix A

Cycling Organizations

American International Cycle Club
P. O. Box 96
Silver Springs, Maryland 20907

American Youth Hostels
National Campus
Delaplane, Virginia 22025

Organizes cycle tours to Britain, among other places.
Accompanied by leaders.

British Cycling Federation
26 Park Crescent
London, England W1N 4BE

The major racing and touring organization in Britain.

Canadian Youth Hostels Association
268 First Avenue
Ottawa, Ontario
Canada

Cyclists' Touring Club
Cotterell House
69 Meadrow
Godalming, Surrey
England GU7 3HS

Oldest and most important touring club in Britain.

International Bicycle Touring Society
846 Prospect Street
La Jolla, California 92037

Organizes first-class bicycle tours in this country and abroad, including Britain.

League of American Wheelmen
19 South Bothwell
Palatine, Illinois 60067

Rough Stuff Fellowship
H. G. Robson
25 Spring Terrace
North Shields, Northumberland
England

Vegetarian Cycling and Athletic Club
Ralph Platt
18a Mill Lane
London, England NW6 1NS

Youth Hostels Association
Trevelyan House
8 St. Stephen's Hill
St. Albans, Hertfordshire
England AL1 2DY

Outdoor Organizations and Other Sources of Information

Automobile Association
Fanum House
Leicester Square
London, England WC2H 7LY

British Mountaineering Council
Room 314
26 Park Crescent
London, England W1N 4BE

British Tourist Authority:

   680 Fifth Avenue
   New York, New York 10019

   John Hancock Center (Suite 2450)
   875 North Michigan Avenue
   Chicago, Illinois 60611

612 South Flower
Los Angeles, California 90017

151 Bloor Street West
Toronto, Ontario
Canada

602 West Hastings Street
Vancouver, British Columbia
Canada

64 St. James Street
London, England SW1A 1NF

Britrail Travel International
270 Madison Avenue
New York, New York 10016

Camping Club of Great Britain
11 Lower Grosvenor Place
London, England SW1W 0EY

Countryside Commission
1 Cambridge Gate
Regent's Park
London, England NW1 4JY

Oversees national parks and long-distance footpaths.

CTC Travel
13 Spring Street
London, England W2 3RA

Travel agency run by the Cyclists' Touring Club. Near Paddington Station.

Department of the Environment
2 Marsham Street
London, England SW1P 3EB

Maintains "ancient monuments," among other things.

Forestry Commission
25 Savile Row
London, England W1X 2AY

Irish Tourist Board
590 Fifth Avenue
New York, New York 10036

National Trust
42 Queen Anne's Gate
London, England SW1H 9AS

A private organization that preserves land, houses, gardens, etc.

Nature Conservancy
19 Belgrave Square
London, England SW1X 8PY

Maintains nature reserves, parks and trails.

Ramblers' Association
1/4 Crawford Mews
York Street
London, England W1H 1PT

Organization of hikers and country lovers.

Royal Society for the Protection of Birds
The Lodge
Sandy, Bedfordshire
England

Maintains bird sanctuaries and observatories.

Scottish Tourist Board
23 Ravelston Terrace
Edinburgh, Scotland EH4 1TA

Wales Tourist Board
Welcome House
High Street
Llandaff, Cardiff
Wales CF5 2YZ

Appendix C

Map Sources

John Bartholomew and Son
Duncan Street
Edinburgh, Scotland EH9 1TA

Bartholomew's half-inch (or metric 1:100,000) maps are best for cycling.

Cyclists' Touring Club
(See Appendix A for address)

Mail-order map service for members.

Ordnance Survey
Department 95/D
Romsey Road
Maybush, Southampton
England SO9 4DH

Government-produced maps of high quality.

Edward Stanford, Ltd.
12-14 Long Acre
London, England WC2E 9LP

One of the largest map shops in the world.

Appendix D

Some English Bicycle Makers, Sellers and Suppliers

Tom Bromwich
140 Far Gosford Street
Coventry, Warwickshire

Good, moderately priced bikes.

Carlton Cycles, Ltd.
Worksop
Nottinghamshire

H. W. Carradice
North Street
Nelson, Lancashire BB9 7 NF

Makers of saddle and pannier bags.

Condor Cycles
90 Gray's Inn Road
London WC1

Central London shop tending toward high end of
price scale.

Dawes Cycles, Ltd.
Wharf Road
Tyseley, Birmingham
Warwickshire B11 2EA

Sturdy, moderately priced, factory-produced touring
bikes.

F. W. Evans
44-46 Kennington Road
London SE1

Good stock of cycles, parts, clothing. Near Water-
loo Station.

Holdsworth
132 Lower Richmond Road
Putney, London SW15

Cycles from moderately priced knockabouts to the
best custom frames. Excellent stock of accessories,
parts, shoes, clothing. (Take London Underground
to Putney Bridge station, then ask directions.)

Bob Jackson
148 Harehills Lane
Leeds LS8 5BD

Fine custom frames.

Jackson's
1 Portsmouth Road
Guildford, Surrey

Karrimor
19 Avenue Parade
Accrington, Lancashire

Makers of saddle and pannier bags.

Ron Kitching
Hookstone Park
Harrogate, Yorkshire

Large shop with big mail-order business.

Cliff Pratt, Ltd.
84 Spring Bank
Hull, Yorkshire

Cycle shop run by an old stalwart of the CTC.

R. E. W. Reynolds
159-161 Wellingborough Road
Northampton NN1 4DX

Moderately priced through custom frames.

C. S. Russell (York) Ltd.
Clifford Street
York

Large stock of ready-to-ride bikes. Similar to a big American bike shop.

Savile's Cycle Stores, Ltd.
97/99 Battersea Rise
London SW11 1HW

Large stock of ready-to-ride bikes. Rental bikes also available.

Jack Taylor
Church Road
Stockton-on-Tees, Durham

Fine custom frames, especially tandems.

Witcomb
25 Tanners Hill
Deptford, London SE8

Moderately priced utility bikes through fine custom frames. (Take London Underground or British Rail to New Cross station; walk east and ask directions.)

Mail-Order Outdoor Equipment Suppliers

Bellwether
1161 Mission Street
San Francisco, California 94103

Makers of light nylon bicycle touring bags.

Bikecology
Dept. W3006
Wilshire Boulevard
Santa Monica, California 90403

Send one dollar for catalog.

Cannondale Corporation
35 Pulaski Street
Stamford, Connecticut 06902

Makers of light nylon bicycle touring bags.

116 /

Co-op Wilderness Supply
1432 University Avenue
Berkeley, California 94702

Eastern Mountain Sports
Box 9123
1047 Commonwealth Avenue
Boston, Massachusetts 02215

Very large catalog of quality merchandise.

Frostline Kits
452 Burbank Street
Broomfield, Colorado 80020

Sellers of sew-yourself kits for outdoor gear.

Gerry/Outdoor Sports Industries
5450 North Valley Highway
Denver, Colorado 80216

Holubar
Box 7
Boulder, Colorado 80302

Sew-yourself kits similar to Frostline products.

Kreeger and Son
Department 34
30 West 46th Street
New York, New York 10036

Moor and Mountain
63 Park Street
Andover, Massachusetts 01810

Sierra Designs
Fourth and Addison Streets
Berkeley, California 94710

Makers of good down clothing and other equipment.

The Touring Cyclist Shop
P.O. Box 4009 BW
Boulder, Colorado 80302

Catalog is small, but items are carefully chosen with
the cycletourist in mind.

APPENDIX F

Gear Table

(for 27″ wheel, rounded to nearest whole number)

NUMBER OF TEETH IN REAR SPROCKET

NUMBER OF TEETH IN CHAINWHEEL	14	15	16	17	18	19	20	21	22	23	24	25	26	27	28	29	30	31	32	33	34
26	50	47	44	41	39	37	35	33	32	31	29	28	27	26	25	24	23.4	22.6	22	21.3	20.6
28	54	50	47	44	42	40	38	36	34	33	32	30	29	28	27	26	25	24	23.6	22.9	22.2
30	58	54	51	48	45	43	41	39	37	35	34	32	31	30	29	28	27	26	25	24.5	23.8
32	62	58	54	51	48	46	43	41	39	38	36	35	33	32	31	30	29	28	27	26	25
34	66	61	57	54	51	48	46	44	42	40	38	37	35	34	33	32	31	30	29	28	27
36	69	65	61	57	54	51	49	46	44	42	41	39	37	36	35	34	32	31	30	29.5	28.6
38	73	68	64	60	57	54	51	49	47	45	43	41	40	38	37	35	34	33	32	31	30
40	77	72	68	64	60	57	54	51	49	47	45	43	41	40	39	37	36	35	34	33	32
42	81	76	71	67	63	60	57	54	52	49	47	45	43	42	41	39	38	37	35.4	34	33
44	85	79	74	70	66	63	60	57	54	52	50	48	46	44	42	41	40	38	37	36	35
45	87	81	76	72	68	64	61	58	55	53	51	49	47	45	43	42	40.5	39	38	37	36
46	89	83	77	73	69	65	62	59	57	54	52	50	47	46	44	43	41	40	39	38	37
47	91	85	79	74	71	67	63	60	58	55	53	51	49	47	45	44	42	41	40	39	37.3
48	93	86	81	76	72	68	65	62	59	56	54	52	50	48	46	45	43	42	41	39.3	38
49	95	88	83	78	74	70	66	63	60	58	55	53	51	49	47	46	44	43	41.3	40	39
50	96	90	84	79	75	71	68	64	61	59	56	54	52	50	48	47	45	43.5	42	41	40
51	98	92	86	81	77	73	69	66	63	60	57	55	53	51	49	47.5	46	44	43	42	41
52	100	94	88	83	78	74	70	67	64	61	59	56	54	52	50	48	47	45	44	43	41.3

Appendix G

Suggested Reading

Alderson, Frederick. *England by Bicycle*. David and
     Charles, 1975.

Defoe, Daniel. *A Tour Through England and Wales*.
     J. M. Dent & Sons, 1959.

Fleure, H. J. and M. Davies. *A Natural History of
     Man in Britain*. Collins, 1971.

Grigson, Geoffrey. *The Shell Country Book*. J. M.
     Dent & Sons, 1962.

Hillaby, John. *Walk Through Britain*. Houghton-
     Mifflin, 1969.

Hoskins, W. G. *The Making of the English Land-
     scape*. Penguin, 1971.

Hudson, William H. *Afoot in England*. AMS Press,
     1968.

Jefferies, Richard. *Field and Hedgerow*. Longmans,
     Green & Co., 1907.

Kidson, Peter, et al. *A History of English Architecture*. Penguin, 1965.

Sloane, Eugene. *The New Complete Book of Bicycling*. Simon and Schuster, 1974.

Teale, Edwin Way. *Springtime in Britain*. Dodd, Mead & Co., 1970.

Index